D1296754

DATE DUE

MAR 1 2 2009		
MAR 2 5 2009		
JUL 2 9 2009		
NOV 1 3 2009		
ILL 7.7.10		
JAN 2 2015		

Library Store #47-0108 Peel Off Pressure Sensitive

Freelance Writing

for Greeting Card Companies

2nd Edition

by

Patrisha Stauss, M.A.

B&S Productions
P.O. Box 418174
Sacramento, CA 95841

Bloomington, IN Milton Keynes, UK
authorHOUSE

AuthorHouse™
1663 Liberty Drive, Suite 200
Bloomington, IN 47403
www.authorhouse.com
Phone: 1-800-839-8640

AuthorHouse™ UK Ltd.
500 Avebury Boulevard
Central Milton Keynes, MK9 2BE
www.authorhouse.co.uk
Phone: 08001974150

First published by AuthorHouse 2/7/2007

ISBN: 978-1-4259-2698-4 (sc)

Library of Congress Control Number: 2006902561

Printed in the United States of America
Bloomington, Indiana

This book is printed on acid-free paper.

Stauss, Patrisha, 1955
        Freelance Writing for Greeting Card Companies
        2nd Edition
        Includes Index

Dismissal of excuses
and obstacles will show how
quick and easy your desires
can be obtained.

This and all enclosed passages by Ronny B.

Patrisha Stauss

TABLE OF CONTENTS

INTRODUCTION

The first *Freelance Writing for Greeting Card Companies* book was written to show a writer how to enter the greeting card market. The book was an introduction for freelance writers to understand the business side of writing for greeting card companies. The writer was guided step-by-step through the process of professionally preparing and submitting material to publishers and editors as well as what it takes to start a small greeting card business. The *Freelance Writing for Greeting Card Companies*, 2nd Edition, is an updated version of the first book, which includes the use of Internet search engines to locate web sites that contain a wealth of information for freelance writers. The 2nd Edition also targets pertinent information every writer needs to know in regards to being self-employed and/or start a small business. The 2nd Edition also includes the addition of two chapters. One chapter is dedicated to resources and the other chapter is designed specifically as a freelance writer's checklist. The expansion of this book provides the updates needed for the writer of today to meet the demand of the greeting card market.

Writing is a good form of self-expression. What better place to have your writing be viewed than in greeting cards? With this genre, you are expressing your own thoughts at the same time you are helping others express how they feel. This is possible because many find it difficult to say what they feel, and they will buy a greeting card to speak for them.

Having your material reviewed by card companies will be easier than having your work accepted and bought by them. Depending on your experience, this book will help in one or more of the following areas: a) increase your knowledge about the business of freelance writing, b) learn how to professionally prepare and submit material to publishers and editors, c) improve your organizational skills, d) know the tax laws, e) explore the Internet web site search engines, and f) locate various related resources you need as a writer. Remember, if you make your work original, unique, and eye-catching, you will increase your chances of having your material on the market.

If you have written material in the form of poetry, passages, thoughts, or verses, you will be able to use them for greeting cards or other product lines. You may want to consider adding computer graphics, photographs, or illustrations to enhance your chances of grabbing a publisher's or editor's attention.

Whether you are a freelance writer with your own business or working with a greeting card company on a "work for hire" basis, or as an independent contractor, you are considered self-employed according to the state and federal government. Remember, you will be responsible for reporting to the government all income received, as well as pay the state and federal taxes. The tax information chapter will discuss the differences between being self-employed, a sole proprietor, an independent contractor, and a partnership.

By the time you finish reading this book, you will be more aware of the process of contacting agencies, publishers, and editors. You will know how to get and stay organized, be able to professionally prepare your ideas for sale on the market, be familiar with the tax laws, be aware of the many resources available to freelance writers, and know what it takes to start a small business. Finally, you will know what you need to research to become a proficient and successful writer for greeting card companies or be able to own your own greeting card business.

-1-

THE BUSINESS SIDE OF WRITING

Whether you freelance part-time or full-time, you must be prepared to invest some time and money in order to succeed as a freelance writer. It takes more than writing skill for you to be efficient and successful. To give yourself a positive edge over other writers, you must learn to plan your time, stay organized, be critical of your work, and remain aware of the pros and cons of trying to get into the greeting card business. No matter what approach you plan to take to break into the world of writing for greeting card companies, keep in mind of the competition you will face. Plan to know all that you can to develop a unique writing style that publishers and editors will find to be irresistible. The world of freelance writing can now be more approachable for employment via the Internet. The Internet world will also assist a writer in obtaining information or resources about what it takes to be self-employed or a small business owner.

As a serious freelance writer, you should take a professional approach, a process more specifically considered in Chapter 3. In order to look and be professional, you must plan to purchase a high quality computer with access to the Internet, wordprocessing software, and a printer. If you are an illustrator or artist, you would probably include purchasing graphic software, a color printer, and a scanner. You may also want to consider purchasing a fax machine and a color copier. The fax machine is considered an expedient method for written correspondence. If you use the fax machine to communicate with publishers and editors, make sure they are accepting correspondence by fax. Most publishers and editors would rather receive a writer's original material through the United States Postal Service (USPS). The purchase of a copier will eliminate you having to go to a reproduction center every time you need to copy several pages. You should also be prepared to invest in copier paper, ink cartridges, hardware repairs, floppy diskettes and compact discs (CD), if you have a computer CD drive.

An investment of time is also essential. You need to research and get to know the card styles that are sold on the market so that you will know which companies fit your writing style. For example, if you like to write humorous verses, then you should research that area of the market. Be aware of your competition. That awareness will help you to prepare and produce the quality of work a publisher or an editor would like to see. When you look at the cards already on the market, be as critical as if you were the publisher or editor. In fact, you should judge your work (whether a written verse, passage, photograph, or an illustration) with the same critical eye. Further consideration of this topic can be found in Chapter 3.

Before you send your material to a publisher or an editor, you should place a copyright notice on the material, then consider registering it with the Copyright Office. The copyright law will protect your work and officially recognize you as its owner and creator. It endows you with the benefits and privileges which ownership entails, and it establishes the fact that only you can decide how the work is to be used, unless you sell that right. The copyright law gives you particular power in dealing with anyone who wants to market your material. A copyright gives the owner the exclusive right to reproduce, distribute, perform, display, or license his or her work, as well as the derivatives of the work. Copyright work must be original and in a concrete medium of expression. A writer's or artist's work is covered under the copyright law whether or not a copyright notice is shown and even if the works are not registered with the Copyright Office. You should understand fully how to use this power so that you will not lose your ownership.

It is easy to copyright your material, but there are many aspects of the law, which you should know in detail. The more knowledge you have about your rights as owner of your work, the less frustrated you will be if a particular issue arises. If you do not register your work before submitting it to a publisher or an editor, you can do so within five years of its publication. Read more about the copyright law later in this Chapter.

If you have a business name or a personal logo you want to use on your greeting cards, other written works, letterhead, or product lines (e.g., mugs, caps, shirts), you may want to consider registering it as a trademark. Trademarks are distinctive symbols, pictures, or words that sellers affix to their material to distinguish and identify the origin of products. The owner of a trademark has exclusive right to use it on the product it was intended to identify, which is often on related products. Under state law, trademarks are protected as part of the unfair competition law (ways used to confuse the buyer as to who really owns a product). Read more about trademarks later in this Chapter.

No matter what you send and to whom you send it, do it in a business-like fashion. Think about how you would like to receive material; in other words, think as a publisher or an editor does. It's obvious that you need an address before you send your material. Not so obvious is the fact that you need a query letter. This is a brief, yet specific, letter stating that you would like permission to send your material to the company for review. Within the letter you should ask for the writer's, photographer's, and/or illustrator's guidelines. The request for guidelines is for your benefit because you want to send material which the card company can sell. If possible, the address on the letter should consist of an "attention" line stating the name of who is to receive the letter or you can write the attention to "publisher or editor". Be sure you have the correct zip code on the envelope to prevent the return of your letter.

If you can't interest the publisher or editor, you may get a rejection notice in the mail. You can expect to receive "rejection" or "not interested" notices for various reasons. Your submission may be turned down because it does not suit the publisher's or editor's personality, or the work load of the company is too heavy to take on more material, or your subject matter may not fit the company's needs. There are many such reasons over which you have little control.

If you receive many rejections, don't get frustrated to the point of giving up writing. It could take several rejections before that right publisher or editor decides that your writing is the perfect choice for publication. You must develop patience in order to successfully pursue this avenue of freelance writing. If you find that you get tired of being rejected, you may want to consider starting your own greeting card business. This will be discussed in Chapter 3.

Know the Market

The greeting card market is highly competitive; your style must be unique, but not offbeat. In order for you to be competitive with your material, you should familiarize yourself with the type of card company that fits your style. The best place to research card company material is at any store which has a high volume of customers. You can look in the smaller stores, but you will find a greater variety of cards in the larger stores. You can also surf the Internet and look through the online greeting card catalogs to get ideas about what card styles are being published, find addresses for requesting guidelines, and learn about the company to see if it fits your style of writing. The Internet offers a great opportunity for writers to stay on top of the trends and to stay abreast of which card companies are in need of writers. The Internet provides a freelance writer the opportunity to locate small niche markets.

Greeting card publishers have specific guidelines as to the way they want a writer's material submitted for publication, which is based on the size and nature of the company. The guidelines will be specific based on the need and expectation of each publisher or editor. When you research the market, pay attention to current topics, artwork or photographs, size and shape of the cards, and the prices. You should also pay attention to the audience that the cards target: a) age, b) children or adults, c) gender, and d) for a friend, relative, or acquaintance. The purpose of researching each particular area within the market is described below:

Current topics - If you don't stay within the current trends, the publisher or editor you approach may be skeptical of placing your work on the market for fear that few people would buy it. The publisher or editor might believe that your submission wouldn't be profitable for the company because the product does not fit within the company's subject realm. It is also possible for your work to be rejected by the publisher or editor because you did not follow the company's guidelines with regard to the topic(s) and/or style.

Artwork and photographs - Although some card companies will take both your writing and your artwork or photographs, they often take only your writing and use it with illustrations or photographs generated by others. Likewise, a card company might take your artwork or photographs and add verses created by other writers. These others may be company staff or independent freelancers. You can find out what stance the company has on this subject by requesting for guidelines in all areas. The company will let you know its expectations in detail.

Card size and shape - If you have a creative imagination for exploring with various sizes and shapes of greeting cards, be sure to find out which companies will allow you this opportunity. If you find a company which specifies card size and/or shape and you don't fit the other categories mentioned in the guidelines, submit only what is specified. A publisher or an editor is likely to return material to those who did not meet the guidelines. Don't take that chance. If you have such a strong desire to explore your creativity in designing your greeting cards, then continue the search for a company that will allow you that freedom.

Price - Look at the price of a card in relation to the first three previous topics. This will give you an idea of what price your cards may carry. If you're not aware of card prices, you won't be prepared to discuss payment terms appropriately with a publisher or an editor, and you may not know if you can make a profit.

Once you have researched the four areas previously mentioned, you will be ready to write to publishers and editors, impressing them with your work by fitting into their company's card styles. First, you should send a query letter requesting guidelines (discussed later in this section). These will be quite specific. If you do not see a reference to your style in the guidelines of a particular company, you should not submit your material. However, if you believe strongly in some particular work, you may write back and ask if the publisher or editor would consider reviewing your material.

Before you send your work to anyone, for any reason, you should consider the following areas of discussion. You need to decide if you want to sell the rights of your work to a greeting card company or keep your rights (to be discussed further in Chapter 2). If you decide to keep your rights, you may want to consider registering your work with the Copyright Office. The copyright information in this book will be referenced toward writers, illustrators, and photographers.

How to Copyright and Register Your Work

As previously mentioned, the copyright law will protect your work and recognize you as the owner and creator of "original works of authorship." You will have the benefits and privileges that ownership entails to both published and unpublished works. When you register your work with the Copyright Office, you will gain more legal power in dealing with someone that infringes on your copyright. Minors may claim a copyright, but state laws may regulate their business dealings. For further information regarding minors and the state laws, or any other information regarding the copyright law, write to:

Library of Congress
Register of Copyrights
101 Independence Avenue, S.E
Washington, D.C. 20559-6000

Visit the Copyright Office web site at www.copyright.gov for general copyright information, various methods to contact the copyright office, and how to order forms. Forms can be ordered by phone or downloaded from the web site. The web site also provides guidance on how to complete the copyright forms.

When you copyright greeting card verses, you can group them by title and copyright the name of the group. This method will save you money. The copyright fee is the same for one verse or for many verses. You can do the math. You can group your verses by topic (e.g., special occasion, humorous, holiday), gender, age, or style. Use a title that will help you to locate a specific type of card when you need to locate a verse or verses. Remember to copy (for your records) the group of verses and the copyright form you submitted denoting their title.

What is a Copyright?

The law was established to protect the work of the creator; it states that the creator is its exclusive owner. As owner, you are empowered to say how your work is to be used and by whom. The law gives the owner power in dealing with publishers, editors, and anyone else who may want to purchase or use the copyrighted work. As owner, you can authorize others to:

- reproduce the work;

- prepare derivative works based upon the original;

- distribute copies to the public by sale or transfer to ownership; and

- display the work publicly.

You do not have to register your work with the Copyright Office to show legal ownership. If you do register your work, you will have certain advantages beyond just the show of copyright. You must register the work before you can go to court in a dispute over rights or ownership. With registration, you can sue for statutory damages and, in addition, recover attorney fees. A registered copyright gives you a stronger case when in court because you have definite proof of your ownership.

If you want to transfer your copyright, it must be stated in writing and signed by the owner of the right in order to be valid. Transfers of copyright are normally through a contract and not required to be recorded through the Copyright Office to be valid. You can contact the Copyright Office for more information on transfer of ownership. When you validate the transfer of ownership through the Copyright Office, it will provide legal advantages. When you transfer ownership, you lose all your rights to the material or work. If a company will not offer to retransfer your rights, you can get them back by serving a written notice forty years after the transfer was made. If the work was published, you can get back the rights thirty-five years after the publication date. Consult the Copyright Office for further information on this issue.

A copyright is subject to the various state laws and regulations governing ownership, inheritance, and transfer of personal property. For information about relevant state laws, you should consult an attorney.

What Can You Copyright?

Copyright protection exists for original works when they become a form of expression, as long as they can be communicated in written, visual, or audio records. Copyright works include the following:

- literary works;

- musical works, including words;

- dramatic works, including music;

- pictorial, graphic, and sculptural works;

- motion pictures and other audio visual works; and

- sound recordings.

The above mentioned are broad categories which consist of subcategories. For the purpose of this book we will cover the areas of literary and pictorial works.

The following categories of material cannot be copyrighted:

- speeches which have not been written;

- titles, names, short phrases and slogans, lettering, coloring, or word and content lists;

- ideas, procedures, methods, systems, processes, concepts, principles, discoveries, or explanations; and

- works of information that are common property for everyone (e.g., calendars, appointment books, and any lists or tables taken from public documents).

Publication of Author's Work and Copyright

The Copyright Act defines "publication" as the distribution of copies of one's work to the public by sale, transfer of ownership, rental, lease, or lending. Publication is an important part of the Copyright because works published in the United States (U.S.) are subject to a mandatory copy of the work with the Library of Congress. You will have to check with the Copyright Office regarding the copyright fee. Publication means:

- a mandatory copy of the work with the Library of Congress;

- the work can affect the limitations on the exclusive rights of the copyright owner;

- the year of publication may determine the duration of the copyright protection; and

- the number of copies of the work for registration of published works differs from registration of unpublished works.

How to Copyright and Register Your Work

You can copyright your work with or without registering with the Copyright Office. You can personally copyright your work with the following notations:

- the symbol ©, or the word "Copyright", or "Copr";

- the year of publication; and

- the name of the owner of the works or an abbreviation that the name can be recognized as the designation of the owner. Example: © 2006 P. Stauss.

Some variations are:

- positions of date and name may be reversed;

- date of completion or year of first publication can be omitted if a pictorial or graphic work accompanies text and is reproduced in or on greeting cards, postcards, or stationery; and

- name of the owner can be a full name, an abbreviation, or a generally known alternative designation of the owner.

You should place your copyright notice on a noticeable area of your work. Display of a copyright notice is especially important if you add your work to another work which has not been copyrighted. Not having a copyright notice may result in another trying to claim ownership of your work. You should make it a habit to place the copyright notice on all your unpublished work. No matter how you decide to display your copyright notice, be consistent, so that your work isn't likely to be disputed. The use of the copyright notice is the responsibility of the author and permission is not required from the Copyright Office.

The current law provides a procedure for correcting errors and omissions on copyright notices for published and unpublished works. The omission or error does not automatically invalidate the copyright if the registration for the work has been made before or within five years after the publication date. A reasonable effort has to be made to correct the error after it has been discovered. Write to the Copyright Office for further information in this area. If you want to send any of your work overseas, you need specific details about international copyright protection. Write to the Copyright Office for international copyright protection information.

Registration and Procedures

The advantages of registration include:

- an established public record;

- the ability to file suit in court, if necessary;

- the protection against importation of infringing copies;

- statutory damages and attorney's fees will be available to the copyright owner within three months after publication;

- if registration is made within five years of publication, establishment of the validity of the copyright; and

- registration can be recorded with the U.S. Customs Service for protection. See the Customs Service web site at www.customs.gov for online publications.

To register your material, the following items should be sent together in one envelope. If any piece of the following is missing, the packet may be returned.

1. An application form;
2. A filing fee; and
3. A copy of the work being registered. The number of copies varies as follows;

    *   If the work is unpublished, one copy of the work.
    *   If the work was first published in the U.S. after 1978, two copies of the best edition
    *   If the work was first published in the U.S. before 1978, two copies of the work as first published.

If sending multiple works, all applications, copies, and fees should be sent in the same package and attach the application to the appropriate copy of the work.

For a small fee, you may obtain more protection by registering your work with the Copyright Office. When you write to the Register of Copyrights, ask for the current fee and the following application forms for literary works and nondramatic works. If you have a computer and a laser printer (a high quality inkjet printer is acceptable), you can find all the information, as well as, print the forms, on the web site at www.copyright.gov.

Form TX: for unpublished or published nondramatic literary works

Form SE: for literary works that would be issued as periodicals such as newspapers, magazines, newsletters, and journals

Form VA: for unpublished or published visual arts: pictorial and graphic

Form CA: to correct or change information sent on an earlier registration form

To register your work, write to: Library of Congress
Register of Copyrights
101 Independence Avenue. S. E.
Washington, D.C. 20559-6000

The Copyright Office does not give legal advice. If you believe information or guidance is needed as a legal matter, you will have to consult an attorney.

Online Information and Fill-in Forms

A writer now has access to fill-in forms and applications on the Internet. You will be able to key in the information on the computer, print the information, and mail it to the Copyright Office. Keep in mind that the Copyright Office prefers all forms and applications be printed back to back on a single sheet of paper. If your printer doesn't have the capability to print double-sided pages from the computer, place your one-sided printed sheet back into the printer and print on the blank side for page 2. You should use 8 ½˝ x 11˝ size paper.

The Copyright Office web site offers the following:

Internet Access: Locate circulars, regulations, other related material, copyright applications, and copyright forms.

Regular
Mail Address: Library of Congress
Register of Copyrights
101 Independence Avenue. S. E.
Washington, D.C. 20559-6000

Fax-On-Demand: Request circulars and publications other than applications with a touch tone telephone.

Telephone: For general information, to request application forms and circulars, TTY, and for the recorded information that is available 24 hours a day.

Online Works: This does not include computer programs and databases. The registration online only pertains to your original works, not any material previously registered, published or in the public domain. The registration has to be limited to the material submitted for copyright on that day received by the Copyright Office. Online material that is updated frequently, a revised version for each revision may be registered separately with a separate filing fee. See the online information on the web site for more information in this area.

Facts About Trademarks

A trademark is a symbol, design, or combination of words or phrases, which identify the source of a product or work and distinguishes it as the material of a particular person from the material of others. A trademark appears in a visible location on the product or on the product's package. A trademark is different from a copyright. A trademark is identifying the source and a copyright of protection for original artist's work or material. Trademarks are powerful symbols that assist businesses in establishing consumer loyalty. Once a trademark is well known because the consumer has adopted your product as a credible item, your other products will likely be searched for by the same consumer or pass the word to other consumers to buy your products.

Before you select, adopt, or use a trademark, you should conduct a professional search to make sure the trademark is not already in use. If someone else has rights to the trademark you have chosen, you could find yourself in a lawsuit. You could also be held liable for monetary damages and legal fees. It is wise to search if the trademark you have chosen is not already registered prior to public exposure to avoid a possible lawsuit.

You do not have to register your trademark because it will be considered yours based on the legitimate use of it. If you choose to not register your trademark, or you plan to register it later, you can only use the "TM" notation, not the ® symbol. The "TM" notation will alert the public to your claim of the trademark. After you register your trademark, only then can you use the ® symbol. Registration of a trademark will protect your business and enable you to maintain an exclusive position in the marketplace for your product. You can establish national rights, obtain nationwide priority, reserve it nationwide, and block others from registering similar trademarks.

Trademark Search

A trademark search will inform you whether someone else already as the rights to your trademark. This search will also let you know that you will have exclusive rights to its use. When you conduct the search, look for all aspects that pertain to your trademark. If the trademark has words and a design, then your search should include the words and the design. Your search should also include federal and state registrations and applications. Someone may have a similar trademark in route to be registered, but had not quite completed the process. To conduct the search, you can go online to the web site www.uspto.gov.

Trademark Registration

When you find out that your trademark is unique, you should file for registration as soon as possible. You never know when someone else has the same idea for a trademark and may already be in the filing process. After the application is received by the Trademark Office, it usually takes six to eight months to determine if your trademark can be registered. If your trademark is determined to not be registerable and is rejected by the Trademark Office, you have six months from the date of mailing to respond or your application will be abandoned. If you believe that your trademark should be registered, you have the right to appeal to the Trademark Trial and Appeal Board. For more information regarding the appeal process go to www.uspto.gov.

If your trademark is acceptable for registration, it will be placed in a weekly publication that lists trademarks seeking registration. This will give third parties, owners of other trademarks, the opportunity to notify the Trademark Office of their opposition to pending trademarks.

The term of a trademark is 10 years and must be renewed at least six months prior to the expiration of its registration. Between the fifth and sixth year following the initial registration date, you must file an affidavit or declaration of continued use with the Trademark Office.

The Application Process

In order for the Trademark Office to accept your application, the following must be included in the packet:

1. Name of the applicant: The name must be the owner of the mark. The owner is the person or entity who is connected with the products identified by the trademark, such as an individual, corporation, partnership, or any type of legal entity.

2. Name and address for correspondence: The Trademark Office will send correspondence to the name and address submitted by the applicant. You must keep your address current with the Trademark Office. Submit a change of address on the web site www.uspto.gov.

   When you send a note to the Commissioner for Trademarks for an address change, place at the top of the paper a heading listing the applicant's name, trademark design, and the application number.

3. Your trademark drawing: You must include a drawing of the trademark you want to register. The Trademark Office files the drawing in the search records, to print in their official listing and on the registration certificate. When you prepare the drawing, use 8 ½˝ x 11˝ white, nonshiny paper with 1 inch margins. The drawing of the trademark should be no larger than 3 ½˝ x 3 ½˝. The drawing page needs to include a heading with the applicant's name, correspondence address, listing of goods and services, date of first use, and date of use in commerce (you can state "Intent to Use Application"). The design of the trademark should appear below the heading, in the middle of the page, and in the proper format for either a "typed" drawing or a "stylized or special form" drawing. After the drawing is submitted to the Trademark Office, you cannot make any future changes.

   A "typed" drawing consists of letters, words, punctuation or diacritical marks and does not include a design or drawing. For this type of drawing, you must write the statement "the mark is presented in standard character format without claim to any particular font style, size, or color." The Trademark Office has created a list of particular letters, numerals, punctuation marks, and diacritical marks that may be used in a "typed" drawing. You may design the trademark in any font style, use bold or italicized letters, and use both uppercase and/or lowercase letters. If you want to register characters that are not on the Trademark Office list, you must file a "special form drawing."

A "stylized or special form drawing" consists of a design or logo. The drawing should show a black and white image and must be an exact representation of the trademark. If you want to use color, you must submit a color drawing. You must also submit a color claim naming the colors and a separate statement describing where the colors are on the trademark. Refer to the web site www.uspto.gov for more information.

4. You must note the specific goods and/or services. You must use common names and language that the general public understands or your application and refund will be returned. After you file the application, you cannot expand or broaden the identification of goods and/or services.

5. The application fee must be included within the packet. The Trademark Office accepts payment by credit card, check, or money order. When the application is given a filing date, the filing fee cannot be refunded.

6. Your application should include your "basis" for filing. The "basis" would state "current use in commerce" or the "intent to use" (for use in the future). If you have started using the trademark in commerce, a "use" based application must include a statement that the trademark is in use in commerce. You would need to list the date of first use of the trademark and the date of its first use in the commerce. The application should include a specimen showing use of the trademark in commerce.

7. A specimen is an actual example of how you are using the mark in commerce. This is not the same as the drawing, which represents what you are claiming as the trademark. A specimen shows the mark on the actual goods or the packaging of the goods. You may submit a label, a container, a display, or a photograph of an item that includes the trademark. Do not submit the actual product. An acceptable specimen which depicts the trademark would include a sign, a brochure about the services, an advertisement for the services, a business card, or stationary showing the mark in connection with the services. The specimen submitted with the application must be flat, no larger than 8 ½″ x 11″.

8. Your signature or someone who is authorized to sign is required.

A registered trademark does not last indefinitely. The owner of the trademark must reregister periodically. Pertinent information regarding filing a trademark and obtaining the forms for filing required documents are available at www.uspto.gov or call the trademark assistance center number located on the web site for further information.

If you prefer to file an application directly over the Internet, you will be able to get online help, the use of a validation function (to assist you in avoiding the omission of important information), an immediate reply via e-mail informing of the application's serial number, a summary of the submission, and 24-hour access (except Saturday 11:00 p.m. to Sunday 6:00 a.m.). The Trademark Office prefers electronic submissions, but you may mail or hand deliver a paper application. You can call the automated telephone line located on the web site to obtain a printed form. You may NOT submit an application by fax.

What Are a Writer's Rights?

This section will define the different rights which empower you to present your work on the market. You should retain as many of these rights as possible. As a beginning writer, you won't be able to negotiate with the publishers or editors as well as one who is more experienced. As you acquire more skill, reliability, and professionalism and the more known your name becomes, you will be considered more valuable to the publishers or editors. Then you will be able to have an edge as to what you expect for your work.

The following are some of the rights publishers and editors seek from writers for greeting card and postcard verses, magazine article submissions, and photographs or illustrations.

All Rights - These are bought by some magazines and greeting card companies. A writer, who sells written work under these terms, forfeits rights of ownership of this material everywhere else. Some editors will work with you, buying all rights for a certain period of time, then let you recover the rights later.

First North American Serial Rights - Magazine companies which distribute their material to the United States and Canada frequently buy these rights. This lets the company be first to use the material in the U.S. and Canada. The writer still owns all other rights.

First Serial Rights - The company will be able to print the work before anyone else is able to do so. All other rights still belong to the writer.

One-Time Rights - The company can use the work only one time, and has no guarantee that it will be first in publishing the material. This right can be used for any kind of material.

Second Serial Rights - A newspaper or magazine has the right to publish material after it has appeared in another publication. The income derived from these rights is usually shared fifty/fifty by the writer and the first publisher.

Electronic Rights (E-Rights) - Rights that cover a broad range of electronic media. A contract should specify if electronic rights are included. Unspecified rights remain with the writer.

- First Electronic Rights - After the material is initially published, you are free to sell your material in any medium.

- One-Time Electronic Rights - Although this doesn't specify a time limit of publication, this allows you to sell your material elsewhere.

- Nonexclusive Electronic Rights - You are allowed to publish your material electronically at any time.

- Exclusive Electronic Rights for Term - A publisher will request to use your material for a certain period of time, then you can reuse the material elsewhere.

Subsidiary Rights - Rights that are covered in a book contract other than the book publication rights (movie, television, audiotape, translation rights, and electronic rights). These rights can belong to the author, the publisher or editor, or both.

Knowing your rights is very important. This is your leverage in dealing with publishers or editors. You want to be in control as much as possible so that you can get the full benefit of the knowledge and experience on which your work is based.

Some greeting card companies buy exclusive rights from authors while others purchase a 24-month market review at which time the company has rights to publish, sell, and promote an author's work for all types of greeting cards, note cards, or any other products. Sometimes publishers or editors won't specify the rights they are buying. If that is the case, then you need to specify what particular rights you're offering (most likely one time or first serial rights).

The Importance of Query Letters

As stated earlier, before you send any material to a greeting card company, you should send a one page query letter. This brief letter introduces you as well as your request for writer's, artist's, illustrator's and/or photographer's submission guidelines. Some companies may have a catalog or market list. You can request the catalog or list, but keep in mind you may not receive one. That's okay, because you are more interested in receiving the submission guidelines. Most greeting card companies are more likely to send you the guidelines if you include a self addressed stamped envelope (SASE). You should also check if the company wants a small fee to send you the requested information. If you have a computer with access to e-mail and you want a shorter turnaround time to your query letter, send it via e-mail. You will have to do a little research on the company's web site and check if they accept e-mail query letters or prefer them by mail service. Treat the e-mail query letter as you would a print query letter; always be professional.

If you send material without permission, you may have it returned or rejected simply because you didn't meet the specific guidelines. It's also possible that the company has gone out of business; find out before you send a costly package. When you receive the guidelines, the best advice is this: follow them exactly. Some publishers require that their guidelines be followed precisely; that's why they have established them for presentation to those who inquire.

A query letter for greeting cards is much different from query letters for book manuscripts, magazine articles, and short stories. The main purpose for a query letter for greeting card companies is to request their guidelines; therefore, you only need to include the basic information as shown below.

A query letter should consist of:

- your name, address, (phone number, e-mail address optional)
- date letter mailed
- greeting card company address
- an attention line for a specific contact person or department (if applicable)
- your intent of the letter
- your name typed with a space for your signature
- a statement to indicate the enclosure of a self-addressed stamped envelope (SASE)

The letter should have a balanced format and be organized. In other words, margins should be set so that the letter is centered on the page. If the letter is not centered, adjust it be a bit higher on the page, rather than too low. A sample query letter follows at the end of this section.

Attaching a brief biography (no longer than one page) is an added touch which might interest a publisher or editor. It should consist of pertinent information relating to the type of material you want to submit. Information which is not relevant is likely to cause a publisher or editor to stop reading, viewing the material as useless in evaluating your potential.

Writers often get anxious, impatient, and/or unsettled if they don't receive the submission guidelines shortly after the query letter. This is not a reason to call the company, get discouraged, or think you have been rejected, although, you haven't submitted your material. The letter may not have reached its destination or the company may have a time frame in answering query letters. The first thing you should do is check that you mailed the letter to the correct address (you should have done this prior to mailing it). If the address is correct and you haven't received your submission guidelines after one month, you can send a follow-up query letter. If you still don't receive a response after another month has passed, you should note in your file that you didn't receive a response then consider sending a query letter to another company. It is a good idea to note when you do and don't get responses from each company so you don't waste your and their time with another query letter process.

Some writers send a query letter to several companies at the same time, then later, note who did and didn't respond and only work with the companies who responded. Some writers never send a follow-up letter to the first query letter, nor do they bother with the worry of not getting that initial response from any particular company. That type of attitude means less stress for the writer and more energy to concentrate on working with a company who is interested in working with them.

Patrisha Stauss
0101 Writer's Lane
Book Path, California 11111
101-222-3456

November 1, 2005

ABC Publishing Company
2222 Editors Street
Writers City, New York 00000

Dear Sir or Madam *(write the person's name or the department if known)*:

My name is Patrisha Stauss. I have written various types of greeting card verses. *(this is the place to mention what types of cards you write, such as humorous, special occasion, sentimental)*

Please send me your writer's and illustrator's submission guidelines. If possible, please include your company catalog. You can send the material to the above address.

Thank you for your time.

Sincerely,

Patrisha Stauss

Patrisha Stauss
pstauss@email.net

Enclosure: SASE

SAMPLE QUERY LETTER

-2-

GREETING CARD COMPANIES

The query letter is the beginning of you selling yourself as a professional freelance writer. If you can obtain permission to send your work to a greeting card company, you then have the task of impressing upon the publisher or editor the fact that you are capable of meeting required standards for making money for the company. Creating that impression will be the deciding factor as to whether you have the talent and experience the company wants. You may think that you will be able to sell your material to a publisher or editor if you receive permission to send your work. Don't get your hopes up until you see a letter accepting your material and stating that a contract or release form will be mailed to you. Although you were asked to send your work, it can still be rejected for a variety of reasons. Remain alert to all of the company's angles and expectations by reading the guidelines carefully, thus decreasing the likelihood of getting a rejection notice.

You should be aware of the different greeting card categories so that you will know what the company is searching for when they request a particular category. In the eyes of the company, it doesn't look good if you appear to guess at what they want. Leaving such an impression is a sure sign of an amateur writer or of one who doesn't care about the company's needs.

There are three categories of greeting cards:

Traditional Cards - These cards have been around for a long time. This classification addresses events and wishes such as birthday, wedding, get well, sympathy, Christmas, Thanksgiving, Easter, and Mother's and Father's Day events. The verses in these cards have a generalized meaning, yet they are expressed with a sensitive and emotional feeling.

Studio (Contemporary) Cards - This category of cards is the same as the traditional set, but the verses are somewhat different. These verses or passages are geared toward the changing of the times. They have a specific meaning with a message that is non-traditional (a more involved meaning). If you write in this area, pay close attention to what is being sold on the market. What may have been popular last year, may not be so this year.

Alternative Cards - This series of selections includes thank you, promotion, salary raise, divorce, friends, gags, and other non-traditional cards with offbeat or humorous messages. This category has become very popular.

Not only do you need to know the card categories, you also need to be aware of the company's clientele, both buyers and receivers of the cards (e.g., woman to woman, mother to daughter, son to father, friend to friend). When the company has specific guidelines in those particular areas, you need to pay special attention to those requirements for your submission. Many card companies will send you samples of their card line if you request them.

You may have specific ideas about the way you would like to present your material, but the publisher or editor knows what cards will sell. The company guidelines will show you what is expected of a writer. You decide to follow them or not. Don't take the chance of losing the opportunity to work for a company just because you may not like the guidelines. The publisher or editor knows that there are many writers who will comply with their standards. If you like a particular company, or if only a few have answered your query letter, then rearrange your work or style to fit the company guidelines.

Contacting the Company

In order to contact the greeting card companies, you must know where to find the addresses. You should be prepared to spend some time researching the market, determining which company would fit your style. Below is a list of places to conduct your research to locate greeting card company addresses.

Book Stores - There are a few books which specialize in supplying addresses for businesses. Before you buy a book, be sure that it has addresses for greeting card companies. If that category is not listed inside the front or back of the book, check the table of contents. The more information the book can supply you, the more you will benefit from using it. Here is what you look for in determining if the book can be of use: 1) company name, 2) company address, 3) contact person, 4) whether the company will consider the work of freelance writers, 5) what writer's rights they want to obtain, 6) submission time or deadlines for acquiring material from the writer, 7) the company needs and product lines, 8) tips for the writer, and 9) how to contact the publisher or editor.

Libraries - Your library may have the telephone book yellow pages of various cities throughout the United States. In the yellow pages, look under the section of either publishers or greeting card companies. Not all cities will have a listing for greeting card companies. In addition, not all telephone books have the zip codes. You may have to go to the post office or check on the Internet through a search engine to locate the zip codes for the addresses you have obtained. You could also ask a librarian if the library has a zip code book.

Local Stores - Many stores sell a variety of greeting cards. On the back of each card you will find one or more of the following: the publishing company's name, city, state, zip code, and the phone number. Sometimes the cards may be on a rotating stand with a sign on top advertising the company which produced the cards. This advertisement may have the company address.

Magazines - Magazines geared toward the business of writing will have many advertisements near the back cover with a section for greeting card companies that advertise the need for writers. Here they will mention what type of material they seek from the writer.

Internet - You can access a search engine through the Internet and type in "search for greeting card companies" or "greeting card companies." Many links will appear that will take you to greeting card company web sites. The web sites will have their physical address located in one of the following web pages: "home page", "contact us", "privacy policy", "employment opportunities", or at the bottom of the web site front page. You can also access the Internet Yellow Pages through one of the search engines.

After you have obtained all of the company addresses, prepare a query letter. It is advisable to put an attention line on the envelope. After you send the letter, you can expect to wait up to six weeks before you get a reply. Some companies may not answer your query letter, or you may get the letter returned, unopened, because the business no longer exists.

When a letter has been returned to you, first check to see if you have enough postage on it. Then compare the address on the envelope to the one you have listed in your files. You will be able to see if you accidentally wrote something incorrectly in the address. If you made a mistake, readdress the envelope and send it on its way. If the letter was undeliverable, keep it for your records. A discussion pertinent to this matter can be found in Chapter 4.

Expectations of Publishers and Editors

Every greeting card company has their own specific submission guidelines. Those guidelines were written for a particular reason, and the editor will expect the writer to follow the guidelines. It is to your benefit to do so, or you may lose the opportunity for your work to be accepted. The guidelines may state that the company pays a flat fee. Another bit of information may be regarding what type of rights the company may buy. Such facts will give you an idea about how to approach the company's publisher or editor, or about how the company may approach you regarding payment.

Companies differ with regard to unsolicited material: some will review it; others may look it over; and quite a few won't review it at all and may send it back if you have an SASE enclosed.

If you sent your material to a company for review after receiving permission to send it, and after a reasonable period of time you haven't received a reply regarding its status, write a letter inquiring about it. Don't bother trying to call, because you may not be successful in reaching the person who has direct contact with the material. In fact, it is unlikely that you would be able to speak to the publisher or editor. These people are very busy and usually have others helping them with their mail and phone calls. A letter will be more beneficial, because it will allow time for determining the status of your submission.

Once your work has been accepted for sale on the market and you are at the stage of revising or finalizing your material, a publisher or editor will welcome your phone calls. Your phone call will definitely be accepted if you run into problems while working on the specific material requested by the company.

When your submission has been accepted, you should receive a letter stating such. That letter will indicate any further requirements that may be expected from you, in addition to the work which you have already sent to the company. You then must decide whether or not you still want to work for the company. If you do, send a reply letter stating so. You will then receive a contract which may be negotiable, depending on the determination of the company and the stance of the publisher or editor. The company's belief in the marketability of your product will determine how far it will negotiate with you. The more reputable you are, the greater your edge in negotiating. For all the company knows, someone else could be competing for your work. Be careful not to be too stubborn regarding your expectations; you may lose out.

Greeting card companies vary in payment for verses that can be used in cards or other product lines. They may pay per verse, per a set of verses, or very few may pay royalty monies. In addition, you can expect that most card companies will buy all rights; therefore, you will have to decide if you want to only submit your work for a short period of time to get your foot in the door of actually selling your material. Once you have that experience that will be a part of your portfolio, you will later have a better chance to use leverage in payment when you work for other greeting card companies.

Below are some possible expectations from a company regarding the writing aspect of your submission. It is very important that you pay special attention to each area.

3˝ x 5˝ or 4˝ x 6˝ Index Cards - Type one verse centered on the top half of the card and your name and address on the bottom half. At the top right corner, place some kind of code for your reference and record keeping. Place your copyright notice at the bottom left corner. If a photograph or artwork is to be included, tape it on the other side of the card.

Specific Card Line - The types of cards sold on the market could be listed. Examples: birthday, get well, miss you, congratulations, and holidays. This area is important to know because any verse that does not fit the company's needs at that time will be rejected immediately. If a deadline for submission is stated, mark it on the calendar. Don't miss it. Otherwise, you can forget sending further submissions to the company for that year.

Style of Verses - If the company only wants humorous verses, don't send them something sentimental. Many companies will send you examples of their types of verses. If you send them something they do not market, it's a sure bet that it will be rejected. Look to see if the guidelines state the categories of buyers on which the company focuses (such as women to women or friend to friend).

Other Product Lines - This line includes: mugs, buttons, shirts, calendars, post cards, note pads, stationery, and bumper stickers. Your verses may be used for any of these items. Sometimes the company may feel that your verse would be more suitable for one of the above rather than for a greeting card. On the other hand, your verse may be suitable for both the greeting card and another product line.

If the guidelines have not stated a specific format, I suggest the following:

On an 8 ½ ˝ x 11 ˝ piece of paper, type one verse centered. On each sheet, type your name and address on the top left side of the sheet with your copyright notice placed either on the bottom left or right side. It is wise to put some kind of code on the top right side of the sheet for your reference and record keeping. Or, if you prefer, use the 3˝ x 5˝ or 4˝ x 6˝ index card method previously described.

Electronic vs. Paper Greeting Cards

There is not much difference in writing for electronic (online) or print (offline) greeting card companies. They both require the writer to follow the submission guidelines. The acceptance of the writer's work is based on the company's card line needs and the writer's ability to meet those needs. Every writer will have an opinion as to whether it's best to write for online or offline greeting card companies.

For those of you not familiar with the similarities and differences between freelance writing for online and offline greeting cards, check out the following lists that detail those similarities and differences. The list will help you to decide which avenue will be best for you to pursue when working with a publisher or editor.

Electronic (Online) Greeting Cards

Musical (often with choice of music)
Recipient needs computer audio speakers
Animation of graphics and text
E-mail submissions to an editor
Quicker response time from an editor
No postage required
Recipient may need a color printer
Locate the store nearest you
 24 hours a day, 7 days a week
Link e-card company to your web site

Greater exposure of a writer's work
Ability to write online
Stay up-to-date with current trends
Job opportunities are posted
Pay range from exposure only to $150/verse
Easy to find information about companies
Scanner required to e-mail artwork
Ability to check company catalogs,
   submission guidelines, and card lines

Print (Offline) Greeting Cards

View several different card companies
Actually touch and open cards
Limited companies in one location
Few cards are musical
Correspondence by regular mail
Response time may be up to 8 weeks or
   longer

Material can easily get lost in mail
   delivery
Pay postage to deliver material
Recipient can display the card
Ability to submit hands-on dummy card
Payment fee varies from $15-$200 per
   verse
Not all companies have a web site
Not all companies have e-mail

Many of the greeting cards you see in the store have a web site. Make it a habit to check the greeting card section every time you go to a store, and write down the information related to the company. When you are ready to track down the company, access the Internet to use a search engine to locate the company's web site. If there isn't a web site, type in the company name to obtain a mailing address.

Computers offer access to the Internet, which gives access to the use of e-mail. This technology has opened the door for freelance writers and artists. Information about the card companies can be located easier, quicker, and at anytime of the day or night, seven days a week. Response time between the writer and the publisher or editor has been shortened to a matter of hours or days instead of weeks or months. A writer will also be able to track the changing trends and check the current submission guidelines. Postage could be eliminated. Many web sites offer a facts and questions (FAQ) page so you won't have to wait for someone to return your call, letter, or e-mail. You may find your answer quickly, and if not, you can then complete the company's online form in order to get assistance from someone. Use the Internet to your advantage. If you don't know how to use a computer, surf the Internet, or use the e-mail, ask someone to show you how.

Some web sites will offer chat rooms, bulletin boards, or forums so writers can communicate with other writers. This type of networking is ideal for finding answers or obtaining valuable information about a company, organizations, writing groups, and available resources.

Selling Your Rights

Keep as many of your rights as possible. In some cases, a writer may have little say about the rights sold to the publisher or editor. If a beginner writer says, "No," too many times, the publisher or editor may eventually stop contacting the writer. A publisher or editor knows that there are many writers who will comply with the company's requests; they may not want to bother with one who won't "go along."

The best way to decide what rights you should sell is to take a look at your material and determine if and how you could resale it with other products on the market. The writer's most important right is to publish the material and the other rights are called subsidiary rights. When it comes to which rights to sell, which are negotiable, and which ones to keep, a writer needs to know the rights that will benefit him or her the most. Publishers or editors like to obtain the book club rights, second serial rights, and reprint rights. They may be willing to negotiate the other rights.

If you sell all rights of your copyright, you can terminate the transfer of rights forty years after the sale or thirty-five years after publication, whichever comes first.

Whatever you do with your rights, the agreement should be presented in writing. Be sure you understand the terms that you are being offered. If the offer is not put in writing by the company, you should present your understanding of your expectations from the company, in writing and send it to the publisher or editor. Remember that there is sometimes a turnover in such positions as publisher and editor, and the rights purchased may also change at that time. An agreement should always be stated in writing to prevent any such changes.

-3-

A PROFESSIONAL APPROACH

The professional approach requires, in addition to the elements previously discussed, a professional manner in presenting your material. Since this step will be the final deciding factor for your work to sell, be sure that the material is compiled as though it were your finest work.

The material you send to a publisher or editor should be your own style; therefore, think of an eye-catching format, unless the guidelines don't give you the opportunity to do so. Put yourself in the chair of someone having to review the material. Try to be objective about your material, and treat it as though you were the publisher or editor reviewing someone else's work for possible publication.

If you want to add designs, artwork, or photographs to your work, check the card company guidelines as to whether they would consider the artwork. The specific requirements would then be stated. If the company supplies its own illustrations, try to get examples of its work so that you can produce your written material according to the style of its card line.

Before and during the time you critique your work, check for errors and make any other necessary changes. When you critique your work, critique it as though it belonged to someone else and you were going to market it yourself. The best test you can put on yourself is to decide if you would buy it. If the answer is, "No," go back to the drawing board.

You can expect some "rejection" or "not interested" notices. This may not be a reflection on your work, especially if the company hasn't reviewed it. There are several reasons why your material may not be accepted. Some of them will be discussed in a later Chapter. Do not get frustrated and ready to quit writing because of a few rejections. Everyone goes through this, and everyone can learn from the experience. If your work is returned without being reviewed, send it to another company. If it has been reviewed and rejected, you have two alternatives: 1) send different material to that company, if the rejection letter invites you to do so, or 2) send the same material to another company which has indicated a willingness to review your work.

Make the Best of the "First Impression"

Now, I would like to help you to improve your techniques for writing, formatting, preparing, and presenting your material. I will give you some ideas as to how you can look professional to any publisher or editor.

Remember that your first step is to check the guidelines to see whether the card company wants you to be specific in submitting your verses or passages. Once you have met their specifications, you can add your touch of professionalism.

Before you submit your material, read the following to make the verses look professional. Some of the suggestions stated below may seem simple, trifle, or insignificant, but to a publisher or editor they are as important as the verses you want them to consider publishing.

Paper - Use quality paper, not erasable bond. If possible, print on a soft tan, gray or off-white colored paper. Never send your work on paper that is torn, wrinkled, or mutilated. Be sure that the paper is clean of unwanted marks.

Ink - Whether you use a typewriter or a computer, be sure that the ink is dark and the printing is even. Black ink is preferable. The letters should be legible and not smeared.

Font Style - Study the style of font used by the companies that you would like to send your material. If a company seems to like a variety of fancy font style, try to send them something unique. Some companies prefer a standard font; to these, you would do well to send them exactly that - with minimal changes in font style. A standard font style is Arial, Courier, or Times Roman. Preferred font size is 11 or 12 point.

Verse Length - Some companies will prefer a particular length for their verses. If the guidelines do not mention this, take a look at the cards sold in stores or on the web site. Stay close to the company's preference. State, if needed, which part of the verse should be on the outside and the inside of the card (this method will be discussed in a later Chapter).

Other Product Lines - If you would like to use your verse on another product line instead of in a greeting card, you should state this in a letter with your submission. It is best to have these verses separated from the greeting card verses if you are sending them at the same time. Be specific as to how the verse is to be printed or presented on the item.

Error Free - Always look over your verses at least three times. This is a precaution; you may see an error you overlooked in the previous review. Read cautiously. Publishers and editors know that everyone can make a mistake, but some extremely noticeable errors cannot be overlooked.

Proof Your Work - If you make copies of your work, make sure the copies are not crooked on the paper, free of unwanted lines or marks, and looks as professional as the original.

If you are conscious of all of the areas above, applying some, if not all of the suggestions, you will have a good chance of receiving a publisher's or editor's positive response toward your work.

The verses should be written in a compact type of format, short and to the point, yet meaningful. Focus on whom the card will be written to and whether the reader will feel that the card was meant especially for them. Greeting cards are used for personal interaction; therefore, the writer has the obligation to make sure the verses have that personal touch. When someone buys a card, there is a hope that the card will have those words that were so difficult to say to someone else.

Not all greeting cards have verses and not all cards rhyme. By the time you finish researching the card styles of a company, you will have a definite feel of what the company likes. If you write best in rhymed verse, look for the company that wants that style of writing. Don't force yourself to write in an uncomfortable style. You know how you write best. It is just as important to locate a company that fits your style as well as you fit theirs. Don't compromise your type of writing style too much; otherwise, you won't be able to effectively express your thoughts.

When you write or design your cards, picture yourself buying the card. Ask yourself if you would buy the card and if it portrays what someone else may want to actually say to another person. If your answer is yes, continue with your work. If the answer is no, stop and take a different approach in the design or verse.

Using Photographs and Illustrations

If you have other artistic talents, such as photography, illustrating, and computer graphics and you would like to use them with your verses, this section will hold valuable information for you. Before you submit any piece of artwork, be sure that the company has stated its approval in the guidelines. It may be better for you to send your artwork without a verse. That's permissible if the company will accept it.

Let's assume that the company would like to see your artwork. The following are some specifications a greeting card company may want to see.

Photographs - Camera ready is preferable. The photograph will be accepted in one or more of the following formats as stated in the guidelines: slides/transparencies, color prints (various sizes), black and white prints (various sizes), or contact sheets and negatives (upon request only). If a caption is to be used on the photograph, there should be enough space for the words. If a theme exists, a notation on the photograph should be provided.

Illustrations - Camera ready is preferable. The work should be geared toward a specific design, season, or holiday. Card specification for the artwork may be mentioned as well as the type of paper preference. Finished artwork might have to allow for bleed where appropriate. If illustrations are cut and taped or pasted on the paper, copy it and check for any shadows that need to be covered, then recopy the sheet.

If words are to cover part of a photograph, be sure to provide enough space (e.g., open sky area or off-center from the subject). The background of the photograph should be either a light or very dark color. Black ink can be printed on the light-colored area and white ink can be used on the dark area. If you want to use colored ink, it's best to do so on a dark area in the photograph.

By law, if a person is the main subject in the photograph, you will need his or her permission in order to sell the photograph on the market. You will need a photo release form signed by that person giving you permission to use it for sale. A photo release will protect you from an invasion of privacy or a publicity law suit. A release is a contract that grants you permission to use the photograph as you wish. An example of a photo release form (for an adult and a minor) will be shown later.

When you type your release form, keep in mind that there are specific legalities which apply to the way the release form is stated. It is advisable to add what may be your purpose for using the photograph; otherwise, you will not be able to use it. If at any time you want to use the photograph in a manner not stated in the release form, you can revise it later, present it to the person to be signed, and file the new release form with the previous release form. Do not throw away the previous release form. The following information is recommended to be stated in the release form.

- whether the person is a child (minor) or an adult (over 18 years old)

- allow to use the photograph for sale and reproduction in any medium purposes for advertising, greeting cards, display, Internet, or various product lines

- allow to altar, modify, or manipulation of the image

- signature of person giving permission for the photo release

- guardian signature for minor

- it states "for valuable consideration" given by both parties to make the release form a binding legal contract

- state the photograph will not be used for the purpose of ridicule, scandal, scorn, indignity, or pornographic viewing

A photo release does not mean you have to pay the person. It is a form of a contract which gives you permission to use the photograph without thoughts of being sued. If the person wants to get paid or you offer to pay the person that would be between the two of you. If you want to use the person on a regular paying basis, that would entail a different contract pertaining to royalty payments. You can find out more about independent contracts in the "Start Your Own Greeting Card Business" section later in this Chapter.

When you have taken a photograph and a number of people, happen to be in the background, don't worry about the model release form if their faces cannot be distinguished. Those people were not the main subject of the photograph. They just happen to have been caught in the camera lens.

The following is an example of a photo release form:

Ms. Photographer
0101 Writer's Land
Book Path, California, 55555
(916) 111-0000

PHOTO RELEASE

In consideration for value, I give permission and authority to Ms. Photographer and parties in connection with Ms. Photographer, the irrevocable right to use my photograph for sale and reproduction in any medium. Ms. Photographer has my permission to copyright, publish, use and reuse such photographs in any and all medium now known or hereafter devised, worldwide, for advertising, greeting cards, product lines, promotion, trade, exhibition, distribution, on the Internet, or any other lawful purpose whatsoever.

I agree that Ms. Photographer may make use of all or any part of the photographs and may alter or modify them. I hereby waive any right to inspect or approve the finished product for advertising. I release Ms. Photographer from any and all liability arising out of the use of the photographs. I agree not to make any claim against Ms. Photographer as a result of the use of the photographs, including, without limitation, any claim that such use invades any right of privacy and/or publicity, defamation, libel, scandal, pornography, ridicule, scorn, and any other personal and/or property right. I am aware that this is a binding legal document.

Please check and initial one of the following:

_____I hereby acknowledge and represent that I am over the age of eighteen years and that I have read and understand this release.

_____I hereby acknowledge and represent that the person photographed is a minor and that I am the parent or duly authorized representative and that I have read and understand this release.

Print Name:_____ Date:_____

Signature:_____

Address (optional):_____

_____

Print Name (guardian of minor):_____ Date:_____

Signature (guardian of minor):_____

Material Submission Organization

To prevent your work from getting lost once it reaches the company, it should have your name, address, phone number, an ID code (see "Expectations of Publishers and Editors" section in Chapter 2 and the "Record Keeping" section in Chapter 4) for reference and your copyright notice displayed in whichever format you use below.

Greeting Card Verses - On 3 x 5 or 4 x 6 index cards, place the personal information, ID code, and copyright notice on the front (preferably) below the verse. If you don't have room for it on the front, place it on the back; it will still be acceptable. If you choose the latter, note it in a letter to the company.

Individual Greeting Card Verses - On 8 ½ x 11 paper, you can present your personal information, ID code, and copyright notice in one of two ways. Place the information on each sheet (front or back), or staple all sheets together and attach a cover letter with your information.

Multiple Verses - If you want to take the time and have access to a binding machine, you can bind the cards or the sheets of paper containing the verses. With this format, you should add a cover sheet that introduces and identifies your material.

Photograph Book - If you would like to get more elaborate, you can place your work inside a photograph book, displaying your identifying information on the front cover. Don't use an album which might make it difficult for the publisher or editor to take out the material.

Photographs - Put all your information on a 3 x 5 index card and tape it to the back of each photograph.

Artwork or Illustrations - Place your identifying information on the back of the sheet. If the writing will show through the paper, you should write the data on a 3 x 5 index card and tape it to the back of the sheet.

Critique Your Work

Now that you have printed your work so that it is appealing to the eye, formatted it for a professional look, copyright protected it, and given it a style all its own, is it complete? Have you gone over it thoroughly enough that you believe it is definitely ready for the market? Are you ready for someone to review and critique your material professionally? Can your work compete with other material on the market? If you say, "No," to any of the questions above, you must critique your work more thoroughly.

The critique of your work (by yourself) will pay off for you financially. The publishers and editors will appreciate your effort. It saves them the time of correcting or reformatting the work. The greeting card company saves money when less time is needed to rework the material.

After you critique your work, you could have others do the same. This would be a good opportunity for you to hear what others think about your writing. When someone critiques your material, treat it as constructive criticism and learn from their opinions. Ask how they might have written or presented what they have examined. It doesn't hurt to listen to suggestions about different ways of presenting your material.

Writing verses of personal, political, emotional, or spiritual expression can be used in or on greeting cards, magazines, mugs, shirts, buttons, calendars, and bumper stickers. What you must do is choose which area that interests you, then engage your talents, experiences, and positive attitude.

If you can reach others through your writing, consider your efforts worthwhile. When people buy your material, they are expressing their approval. They are also telling you to keep on writing and displaying your artwork.

Keep in mind that to critique your work is to look at every aspect of your freelance writing, not just the work you produce. When your material is positively ready to be presented to publishers or editors, you should be able to answer, "Yes," to each of the questions in the first paragraph of this section. Now ask yourself the following questions.

1. Will the card company consider the material as fitting their product line?

2. Will a publisher, editor, or anyone buying the card understand what is being conveyed?

3. Is the typing legible and error-free?

4. Does the material fit the company guidelines?

5. Is the format uniform and consistent?

6. Would I buy my own material?

7. Am I aware of the "rights" the company wants to buy?

8. Does the artwork or photograph fit the written material?

9. Does the artwork or photograph fit the company's guidelines?

10. Does the artwork or photograph look professionally done?

11. Is the material coded for record keeping reference?

12. Is the quality of the work acceptable for sale on the market?

13. Did I copyright the material?

14. Does the material look original?

15. Have I looked over the material enough times to say "Yes," to all of the above questions?

There may be times when you feel that no one could resist your work, yet you get a "rejection" or "not interested" letter. There are a variety of reasons for that kind of response. Don't take the rejection of your work as a personal rejection; see what you can do to make the next submission more acceptable. Before you get upset and want to quit, check all the possible rejection reasons below.

- It's supposed to be a humorous card, but it isn't funny enough.

- The verse doesn't make sense.

- The idea has been overworked.

- The verse is too corny or too cute.

- The material doesn't fit what's being sold on the market.

- Guidelines weren't followed.

- The artwork isn't suitable for the type of verses being written.

- The deadline for the material was missed.

- The company wasn't accepting new material at that time.

- The company doesn't accept unsolicited material.

- You may have asked for the material to be used on an unfamiliar product.

- The publisher or editor has changed, and the material may now not fit the requirements.

- Your expectations could not be met.

If you are lucky (very few are), your rejection letter will include the reason your material wasn't accepted. If you are told the reason, use it as a learning experience to make the correction and not to submit the same "error" to the company that returned it. If you don't agree with the rejection reason, don't change anything. Send the same material to another company that you think will appreciate your efforts. If you are not told why your material was rejected, go down the list I just presented to you and try to determine what you think the reason might have been. If you still can't determine the rejection reason, send the same material to another company. If the same material keeps getting rejected, stop mailing it, and make some changes before you send it out again. Remember that a rejection isn't necessarily saying you "stink" and you should stop trying. That's why when you critique your work, you are looking at every aspect of your writing and the expectations of others.

Start Your Own Greeting Card Business

If you prefer to own a greeting card business, you will need to know the basic facts to get started and stay in business. Remember to apply the techniques, suggestions, and advice you read earlier in the book and what you will read after this section. The knowledge will give you the opportunity to be more "well rounded" as an entrepreneur. By the time you finish reading this section of the book, you will know whether you want to have your own business (all profits go to you), freelance your work for various companies (get paid per idea or set of ideas), or work for a company as an employee (all work belongs to the company, you get paid a salary).

There are advantages and disadvantages to owning your business. Here are a few:

Advantages	Disadvantages
You will be a sole proprietor for tax purposes	You have to do the marketing and selling
Create your own design	You have to be the bookkeeper
Set your own guidelines	Keep track of income & expenses for taxes
You have total control	Finance the whole business or get a loan
Set your own deadlines	Partner up with another artist, then some profits
You can recruit another artist to share in the cost of the business	will be split or royalties paid
Recruit a business partner with different artistic talent	Research who would sell your card line
	Distribute the cards or hire a distributor
Work anytime of the day or night	Purchase equipment for production
Work from your own home	Find a printing company
	Need office space (in or out of home)

If you have determined that you still want to have your own greeting card business, you need to find out if you are required to have a business license and a seller's permit in order to "officially" be considered a business to sell products. The Internal Revenue Service (IRS) may not require that you have the license and the permit, but the state, city, or county government may require you have them.

You can find the licensing department telephone number in the white pages of the telephone book or on the Internet through a search engine.

To locate the licensing department in the telephone book white pages, look in the City Government section in the front of the book and search for licenses, which refers you to businesses; here you will find the phone number. Depending on the type of license you qualify for, you may be able to have your business office out of your home, but there may be a stipulation of no customer traffic allowed in your home. Make sure you know what the stipulations are with the license and whether you may want to rent office space outside of your home where customer traffic is allowed. You will be required to update your license after a certain period of time. The licensing department will let you know when your license will expire. How your home office can be considered for tax purposes will be discussed in the Tax Information Chapter.

For information about obtaining a seller's permit, search in the telephone book white pages and look in the Government section for "State of" and search for the State name (such as California); search for Equalization Board of; search for District Business Office; search for Sales Tax Use and there you will find the location of the phone number. You may be required to have a Seller's Permit if your State requires businesses that sell products to pay sales tax. If you are required to have a Seller's Permit and another business purchases your greeting cards or product lines for resale, they will be responsible for the state sales tax. That business will have to give you a purchase order or a copy of their Reseller's Certificate, which exempts you from having to pay the sales tax. Pay special attention to the resale option because you need to keep track of this method for the end of the year tax time to pay the sales tax if any is due (usually in January).

Since you will be recognized as a business, you will need a business name so your customers will know who is selling those fabulous greeting cards. To be recognized as a business, whether you have a license or not, you will need a fictitious business name. When you contact the County or City Licensing Department, they will be able to send you paperwork to register your business name. After your business name has been accepted, you will be required to advertise the announcement of your business within a particular newspaper for a certain period of time.

Whether you have questions regarding the starting of, maintaining, and/or expanding your business, you can contact the Small Business Association (SBA). The SBA can be located on the Internet at www.sba.gov. The web site is filled with useful information for every small business owner. Be aware that not all the information for small businesses will pertain to your type of business.

You may want to consider building an Internet web site to market your business. As you explore this option, check if you need to purchase a domain name (a unique identifier for your web site). The best way to go about researching this option is to find a web site that offers web hosting services. You can develop your own web site by using the host's web site building tools. Some hosts offer ready-to-use templates or the capability for you to build the web site from "scratch", which means you need to know how to use html codes. Some sites have specialized text that will create a hidden html code, which you can view later for editing purposes. If you don't know how to use html codes to build a web site, go through an Internet search engine and search for web sites that offer free html techniques.

The cost for the use of a hosting web site can range from $0.00 to a few dollars a month. If you are willing to pay for the service, make sure you know what is being offered. Some host web sites offer package deals. If you don't want to build your web site, you can locate some businesses that are willing to provide a web page for your products to be viewed by their members that are partner companies or agencies (buyers). Most of those web sites provide web page templates. Of course, that service will cost you a monthly or yearly fee, possibly to be paid in advance.

Whichever web site method you choose, you will have to consider whether or not you need an e-commerce store, a shopping cart, a secure server for ordering, a merchant account for the acceptance of credit card payments, an e-mail account, and customer contact information. You may find that the hosting web site will offer most of the just mentioned services. Check whether the hosting web site is offering those services for free, as a part of the service charge, or as an extra charge for some or all of the services.

Whether you use your own web site, a hosting web site, or neither, you can advertise and market your products through various types of advertisements through other Internet web site businesses. You can start with a search engine to locate those web sites that will let you advertise in their classifieds section or pay a small amount to advertise on particular pages on their web site. No matter how you decide to market your products, make sure you can offer an e-mail address, a fax number, or a message phone number. You will need a communication avenue for your customers to purchase your products or you may find your sales will be low.

If you hire an independent contractor or work with another freelance writer on an assignment, you should consider writing a contract for service and payment. The contract will be a legal binding document. No matter how much you believe that someone you know is your buddy and nothing could go wrong, you should make it a business habit to have a contract for both parties to sign. That way everything agreed upon is in writing, which can be referred to later if necessary. You can purchase a book, computer software for writing contracts, or go on the Internet and search for "subcontractor contracts" to get samples of how to write contracts along with the pertinent and legal information that should be in them. The sample contracts will consist of legal words, phrases, or sentences, which should be included in your business contract. After you write the contract, you may want an attorney to review it before you and the subcontractor sign it.

In Chapter 6 "Tax Information", you will find examples of tax forms required by the Internal Revenue Service (IRS) and tax laws that are specific to owning your business as a sole proprietor. Chapter 7, "Resources", lists small business services, self-employment information, and various Internet web sites that cater to freelance writers.

-4-

KEEPING YOU AND YOUR

WORK ORGANIZED

The signs of a sound business are good organization, up-to-date filing, and accurate record keeping. I have a three level system for my record keeping process, which I will share in more detail later. This Chapter will describe how to keep you and your work environment organized: 1) supplies, 2) filing, 3) time management, 4) record keeping, 5) accounts receivable and accounts payable, 6) stress management, and 7) business resources. Part of the success of keeping your business organized is keeping yourself organized. This section will explain how to be successful at keeping you and your work environment organized.

The Importance of Being Organized

Not only is being organized a good idea for your benefit, the government will also be interested in your financial situation. When it's time for you to compute your taxes, the government's interest should be considered. If they receive any records of your transactions from other sources, they will be expecting to hear from you. The more organized you are, so will be your record keeping system. This will enable you to spend more time on your freelance work. The way you process your transactions and receipts will be important to your record keeping system.

The supplies you have on hand are also a part of staying organized. It could be very frustrating and time-consuming if you don't have the items when you need them. You could also miss a submission deadline if you have to take the time to go shopping. I always keep more than enough office supplies so that I won't later discover that I don't have enough of something to finish a project. When I see that I am getting low on an item, I plan to purchase extra supplies during the next shopping trip. I suggest that you periodically check your supplies or keep a running list of what is needed. Such a list will prevent you from forgetting what to buy when you arrive at the store.

You should keep track of all transactions in the form of a filing system, whether it is on a computer or in a filing cabinet. If you are able to use a computer and a filing cabinet, one can be used as a back-up to the other.

Time management will be very important in meeting project deadlines. Imagine that it's Thursday night and you are preparing a submission which should arrive at a company on Monday or Tuesday. To have it ready in time, you need to mail the package on Friday. If you do not have the items you need to complete the work on Thursday night, you now have to go to the store on Friday, finish the work, and still try to mail it before the end of the day. If you also work at a regular job, you may have less time to get all of that done. Try to keep readily available all of the items you will need (or extra, if possible) for every aspect of your writing or artwork. The more accessible these things are, the more effective you can be at meeting deadlines.

Your record keeping will consist of tracking: a) accounts receivable, b) accounts payable, c) customer addresses, d) date of submission and location of outgoing projects, e) business expenses, f) tax return forms, g) contracts, h) business forms, i) correspondence, and j) supplies.

Stress management may not seem to be a part of being organized. If you have experienced moments, hours, or days of working under stress, you will find that your work productivity, your efficiency level, and emotional state of mind will have a direct effect on your quality of your work and meeting your deadlines. Knowing how to control and manage stress is an important factor in keeping yourself organized.

You should be aware of the type of mail services available to you. If you know what mail services exist regarding prices, amount of time needed for delivery, how the service is provided, what preparation is needed, and the method of delivery, you can choose the best type of service for sending your material. A company may have suggested a particular mail service that it would like you to use. The more you are aware of the various mail services, you can save time because you planned ahead.

Your business resources should be recognized as the foundation of your capability of obtaining material, advice, or consultation needed to produce your work, as well as the avenue to marketing, distributing, and selling your material to publishers, editors, or customers. You should rate the local community and Internet agency-related resources a high priority to being organized.

Many of you are probably thinking that you're not considered an organized person, and you probably won't be able to be as organized as this book explains. Don't get discouraged. Take a couple of areas as a starting point to begin your journey to get organized. Those of you who are very organized may find one or two suggestions to be of use. The suggestions may even stir other ideas you may find to be useful to help you stay organized. The suggestions are areas for you to explore, manipulate, and implement what works best for you.

Keeping Yourself Organized

Many people think of being organized in relation to record keeping, filing, and paperwork stacked on the desk. Now, that is a good start. Other factors to being organized also encompass , time management, and the work environment. When you combine all of these areas to keeping yourself organized, you will encounter less stress, less frustration, and inherent an overall good feeling of being able to concentrate on completing the task or assignment (and actually meeting the deadline).

Personal Management

When it comes to , only you can determine the best approach to keeping yourself organized, focused, motivated, and ready to meet your (and others') expectations. Now, you may say, "that's easy" or "how will I be able to do that?" You might even think it is odd to focus on . Hopefully I will be able to give you some suggestions to help you implement techniques whether you think you're already successful in this area, need more help, or you're just totally confused about the whole idea.

Start by making a list of your personal strengths and weaknesses. Remember there are no right or wrong answers regarding this process because you are telling yourself about your strengths and weaknesses (which we all have). Don't worry at this point what someone else would consider as your strengths and weaknesses. That discussion will come later. Now, be honest, because you will only be holding yourself back from what could be critical decisions in incorporating the improvements needed for your enhancement. If you find it difficult to rate yourself (and many do), remember that you are the only one who will see the list. When you finish, put the list away for a day or two. Continue doing whatever you have planned, but don't look at the list until you are ready to go forward to work on improving your techniques. Once you decide to look at the list again, I want you to try the following techniques. As you go through the steps, you will find some techniques will take more time to complete than the others. The length of time you work on a technique is up to you. Just remember you are trying to fine tune your . First, ask yourself, "how important is that to me?", then take it from there.

Step 1: Review your list of strengths and weaknesses. Determine whether you need to add, delete, or switch any of the strengths to a weakness or a weakness to a strength. At this point, you are reviewing yourself a second time to really determine what are your strengths and weaknesses. If you don't need to make any changes, that's great. Continue with the next step.

Step 2: Next to each strength and weakness write why you think it is a strength or a weakness. This gets you to thinking about why you view yourself with those particular strengths or weaknesses. You may find it difficult to say why because you aren't use to reviewing yourself, just remember, no one else will know. But, you still need to know why you chose those attributes as your strengths and weaknesses.

Step 3: Now, determine if others would agree with you on your choices of strengths and weaknesses. Highlight those areas others may not agree with you and note why. Determine if it is important to you as to what others think about you.

Step 4: Take your list of finalized strengths and weaknesses and compare it to the areas of what others may think. If you don't care and don't plan on changing how others view you, skip this step and go on to the next step. If it does matter to you, write down what you want to do to improve on your strengths, how to turn a weakness into a strength, or how to use a strength to compensate for a weakness.

Step 5: Now it's time to work on enhancing your strengths and eliminating, changing, ignoring, or compensating for your weaknesses. Mark each weakness as to whether you want to eliminate it, change it, ignore it, or compensate with a strength. Next, review the following explanations that will help you complete this step.

To eliminate a weakness, may take some time. You have decided you don't want it anymore. You may have to eliminate it in stages or in small increments until it is considered to no longer exist. This may be the most difficult area to work on. You will have to determine how important it is to eliminate the weakness so you know how much energy to put into it.

To change a weakness, will require that you turn it into a strength (example, constantly being late could be turned into showing up on time). You may find that not all weaknesses can be changed into a strength. Making changes will require you to constantly be aware of when the weakness is about to occur and that it has to be changed and if you want to work on the change at that time.

Ignoring a weakness is probably the easiest way to handle having the weakness. You just simply ignore it. Just because you ignore the weakness, doesn't mean it won't get in the way. You can always choose to work on the weakness at a later time.

Compensating for a weakness requires you to use a current strength to cover for the weakness (start a task one hour earlier than others do to complete it on time because you need more time to read, write, draw, or whatever else may be the weakness). It may take some time for you to determine what strength can compensate for what weakness.

When you find out what works best in finding the comfort level in dealing with your weaknesses, you will experience less stress, less frustration, and increase your ability to complete tasks. You may also find that simply changing your way of thinking about being organized will be enough to enhance your personal strengths or see some of the weaknesses change into strengths.

Time Management

Organizing your time will allow you to be more efficient and not miss submission deadlines. Use a calendar to mark the deadlines for material submissions. You can use a daily, weekly, or monthly calendar. The calendar can have information regarding the stages of your work (including a completion due date) which you need to have accomplished by specific dates. Appointments and meetings can also be written on the calendar. Check the calendar daily or weekly, depending on the types of assignments you are trying to complete.

Use a "To Do" list. Sometimes I may have ten items to accomplish in a weekend. I write them on a piece of paper and cross them off as I finish each one. I may number the items on the list and work in sequence.

Appointment books are good to use. You don't have to only write business appointments. This is where you want to write what time to work on a project or start a task, when a project has to be completed, when to mail or submit a project, the project due date, when to run errands, or to remember when to do something or call someone.

Use a timer or alarm clock when you need to end one project and start another one. You can also use the timer or alarm clock to let you know when it is time to take or end a break.

A tape recorder can be used to record rather than write what you need to remember. Some people work best with an audio playback than try to write or read the information.

The information can be typed on a computer through a wordprocessing program, a software that produces calendars, a program called Inspiration, or with Microsoft Power Point. Many of the computer programs allow additions of color, sound, graphics, and different font styles so you can be creative in how you manage your time.

You may even think of another way to track your time. Whatever method you use, make sure you use it to its fullest extent. You may even use a variety of techniques to accomplish your tasks and meet all your deadlines.

Stress Management

It is very important that you have a low stress level. Something is always applying stress, and it may often appear hopeless to reduce or eliminate the stress. One thing for sure is that you need to learn to keep your stress level at a minimum. High level of stress can cause anxiety, sleeplessness, tension, frustration, and lack of motivation, which in turn may cause lack of productivity and efficiency.

To relieve stress, try one or several of the following:

1. Take several mini breaks if you need to work on a task for a long period of time.

2. Get enough sleep. You know how long you need to sleep to feel rested.

3. Eat nutritious meals. Keep snack food handy for those emergency hunger pangs.

4. Relax some days for a period of time. Take a small vacation from the work world. The vacation may be in your back yard or spending time with your family and friends.

5. Exercise whenever possible, even if it is for only a few minutes.

6. Evaluate your work area. Determine if it is a place that you can be productive. Some people work best when they play music, eat a snack, move around, sit outside, or work with someone. Make your work environment a pleasant place where you want to work.

7. Always give yourself enough time to work on a project which incorporates some of the above-mentioned stress relievers.

You will find you are more apt to concentrate, be motivated, meet deadlines, and be more creative with less stress in your work world.

Work Environment

Your work environment should allow you to concentrate and include all the things that motivate you to want to work. Everyone can be distracted by someone or something; therefore, you want your work environment to be free of those distractions.

The work environment needs to include all the material, books, information, equipment, and supplies ready and accessible as you need them. Try to find a small bookcase or a table with shelves to hold your material. I like the idea of a bookcase. Along with holding books, it can hold other items such as paper, envelopes, folders, and scissors. All your material should be easily accessible so that you don't have to hunt for anything. The secret is to be organized for efficiency.

Decide where you want to develop your work environment. If you are easily distracted by family or friends, choose a place where they know not to bother you while you are in that location. What do you need to help you concentrate? Do you need music, be near the kitchen, be near a window to see outside or let the sun in, have enough room to move around, or have total silence? You may need to make arrangements for someone to answer the phone when it rings, watch the children, or run those errands that could cause you to procrastinate instead of working.

More Ideas to Be Organized

If you don't have a computer, you will definitely need a typewriter. Get an electric one with a correction feature. Some typewriters have a spell checker, but you still have to read every word and every sentence carefully; do this more than once. Often I will see an error which I missed the first time through. Before you send the material to anyone, check the ink quality, format, and have it error-free.

If you can't afford a file cabinet, you could use a sturdy box. Use manila folders to divide the categories and subcategories. There is no way around it; you will need a filing system. When the greeting card companies begin responding to your inquiries, the filing will accumulate. You will find that many companies are willing to answer your query letter. Never throw away the letters (even rejections); file them so that you are aware of your status with each company. Don't throw information in a box without some organization, save yourself the frustration of having to search through everything for one small piece of information.

Don't allow yourself to procrastinate. Do not be around anyone or anything that easily distracts you from completing a task. You may be able to work while that person is sleeping, at work, or visiting with someone out of the house. If you like to talk on the phone, turn off the ringer and let the answering machine get it. If you like to watch television, turn it off. Send the children to grandma's or the neighbor's house. Send the spouse or significant other to another part of the house or make arrangements to work when that person is gone. If the outside sounds and movement of nature or animals distract you, close the windows or curtains and the doors. You may feel "pinned up", but it is only temporary. Remind yourself and others, these needed changes are only temporary, and you will make it up to them at another time.

You should always use top quality material. Don't settle for second best. It's better to spend a little more money for quality than to lose an assignment. Some companies may like your writing, yet reject your material because of poor quality in a photograph or artwork.

Some writers get someone else to shoot their photographs or illustrate their work because they do not have the time or cannot do the job as well as a professional in that field. The best professional for you to use as a photographer or illustrator is a friend or relative who is willing to wait until you get paid.

Remember to record who helps you with any part of your work. You don't want to forget whom you have to pay and how much. You could develop a contract that both of you will sign. The contract is a legal binding document and proof of what the agreement is between you and the other party.

Record Keeping

There are several stages of record keeping. Record keeping involves, filing, computer entries, incoming and outgoing mail activity, correspondence tracking, and income and expense tracking. I will discuss these areas along with more ideas you may want to incorporate into your own method of record keeping. One of my strengths is staying organized; therefore, I believe I can give you some good advice on how you can become organized or possibly add to your current techniques for being organized.

I use a three-level record keeping system (to be described later step by step). The three-level system consists of: 1) business contact and correspondence letters that I have mailed; 2) a ledger with the company name and the date of all material I mailed or was returned to me; and 3) the accounts payable and receivable ledgers (a list of all transactions which involves money).

Within my writing area, I have a "basket" which consists of material and paperwork to be filed, may require my attention later in the week, incoming and outgoing mail, items I have to read, and anything which requires photocopying. When I receive something, related to my freelance business, I open it upon its arrival. It is imperative that I know if I need to deal with an issue or a bill immediately. If something needs my attention at that moment, I take care of it; otherwise, I put it back in the basket to be sorted later according to the attention needed by me. I check the basket once a week to file the material and enter information in the computer, or place it in a "to do" folder or pile. The "to do" folders or piles are labeled according to what I need to do with each piece of mail or material. The labels may read "make phone calls", "need call back", "to file", "to review", "computer entry", "e-mail correspondence", "do by this date____", plus more categories.

If I receive a rejection notice, I treat it like a normal letter to be filed. It's filed and noted in the computer and on the hard copy as a "rejection notice". I don't want to send any information to the same company twice. Businesses do not appreciate that type of mishap.

Before you submit your material, place an ID code with each verse for record keeping purposes. The ID code should be related to the category or type of verse. You could use any one of the codes below. These are just a few examples; you can easily make up your own.

H15 = "H" stands for humorous; "15" stands for the fifteenth verse written.

S25 = "S" stands for serious; "25" stands for the twenty-fifth verse written.

R10 = "R" stands for religious; "10" stands for the tenth verse written.

XMAS 2 = "XMAS" stands for Christmas; "2" stands for the second verse written.

MOM 6 = "MOM" stands for Mother's Day; "6" stands for the sixth verse written.

Three-Level Filing System

Addresses - This category has different subcategories listed alphabetically by business type. Each subcategory lists the particular addresses of letters or material which I have mailed or received. After each address, are the contact person and the company phone number. When I list the addresses, I write some kind of notation or a symbol to remind me that I have mailed or received something. I use the symbol (#) for noting that I mailed a query letter and the symbol (*) that I received a correspondence from that company. Any other information I may need to know is placed next to the symbol in parentheses.

A Ledger - This is a form which has the following information at the top of each page: company name, description of item(s) mailed, date item was mailed, date item accepted, and date item was returned to me. When I send my card verses (or any other material), I place the information in the ledger. Each page of the ledger has the name of the month during which the activity occurred. Remember that if you have any material returned to you, write a notation within that month of the ledger.

Ledger - Page 1
(September 2005)

Company Name	Description	Date Mailed	Date Accepted	Date Returned
A-1	HG 1,4,7,8	9/13		
Love Greetings	SG 2, 10, 13	9/22		

Ledger - Page 2
(October 2005)

Company Name	Description	Date Mailed	Date Accepted	Date Returned
A-1 Pub	HG 1,4,7,8			10/20
Love Greetings	SG 2, 10, 13		10/26	

Accounts Payable and Receivable - This is another form related to the ledger, except that it shows transactions involving money. The months on this form can be combined unless you have many activities occurring in the same month. It is important to keep these records so that you will be able to track your income and expenses. In the beginning of your business you will not make a profit. When you do begin to make a profit, you will want to know.

If you are not familiar with the terms *Accounts Payable* and *Accounts Receivable,* read the following definitions.

**Accounts
Payable** -   Money you pay for someone's services.

**Accounts
Receivable** -   Money you receive for material you sold.

ACCOUNTS
PAYABLE AND RECEIVABLE
JUNE - AUGUST 2005

Date	Item	Company	Amount Paid	Amount Received
6/18	Card Illus.	Bill Rase	50.00	
7/10	5 cards	Love Greetings		250.00
8/29	Article	Kids Poetry		42.00

Once all the information is entered in the computer, I will do one of two things depending on how hectic my day has been. If I have a slow day, I will process as many items I can for that day. Remember that some of the information you enter in the computer will not be printed. If you have a computer hard drive, save it there and on a floppy disk or a CD. The disk will be your back-up copy. If I'm too busy to file, I will process the computer entries and put the paper copies back into the basket and file them later. You will have to decide how to manage your time. Don't let the basket get too full or let too much time pass before you get to it; waiting too long may cause you to miss a submission deadline.

File Cabinet

A file cabinet should be arranged in alphabetical order by main categories. Within the main categories, you should have subcategories alphabetized. I consider the following to be general main categories. There may be other main topics depending on what you need to be organized.

<u>Main Categories</u>

Accounts Payable/Receivable
Advertisement
Artwork
Copying Services
Business Addresses
Contracts
Copyright Information
Correspondence
Expense Sheets (By Year)

Greeting Card Companies
Invoices (Outstanding and Paid)
Licenses
Marketing
Photography
Printers
Receipts (Current Year)
Resale Certificates
Tax Information

When you are ready to purchase a filing cabinet, set aside some time to research the different styles, sizes, and prices. These days, you have a choice of many varieties. You want to take into consideration the amount of space you have for the cabinet size and style you choose. In addition, you will want to think about your freelance/business future. As you expand your freelance activities and accumulate more equipment and supplies, you will need more space in the computer, in the filing system, and in your work area. Always think ahead when it comes to purchasing supplies, equipment, and work or office space.

Preparing Your Submissions

When you have compiled between ten and fifteen verses, clip them together and send them to the greeting card company (unless the guidelines specify otherwise). This number of verses will give the publisher or editor a variety of ideas from which to choose. The company may accept one to all of the examples to review for the market.

Don't think that all you do is place your material in an envelope and mail it. That simply isn't so! Some company submission guidelines state the way in which you must submit your work. If there aren't any guidelines, you could follow the techniques listed below (SASE means self-addressed, stamped envelope):

- Whatever the size of your submission, always send the greeting card company the same size envelope with the correct postage for return. Along with the #10 envelope, keep other envelope sizes handy: 6" x 9", 8 ½ " x 11", and 9" x 12". Don't forget to write or place your self-stick address label on the stamped return envelope.

- Query letters may be folded and sent in a #10 envelope, unless you send them an SASE. If you do send an SASE, use an 8 ½" x 11" envelope for the query letter and the correct size return envelope. If you are expecting the company to send you information, your return envelope should be either the size 6" x 9" or an 8 ½ " x 11" with enough postage.

- Send all your material First Class mail. That rate will be handled more carefully than Third Class. You will pay more, but it's worth it. If you are close to a deadline, you should consider using Priority Mail. It also costs a little more, but it is suppose to arrive sooner than the First Class mail (or so they say).

- If you have a thick submission, you could place it in a box not much larger than the material. Place your SASE inside the box.

- To send photographs or slides, pack them well and try to send them with the submission. If you have to send them separately, include a cover letter stating exactly what goes with what. Both submissions should be coded for easy matching by the person receiving the mail. Photo mailers can be used to hold the photographs for better protection. Slides should be put in plastic sleeves and packed between cardboard or in a small photo mailer. If you want them back, state in your cover letter that you would like to have the photographs returned. Don't forget the SASE with the correct return postage.

- If your submission is mailed out of the United States, you will have to add extra postage to send it and to have it returned. Some countries will want you to send International Reply Coupons (IRC); check the guidelines. You can obtain IRCs at the post office.

- When photographs/slides are being mailed, write "Photos - Do Not Bend" on the outside of the package. This alerts the postal people and the receiving company to be careful when handling it.

I learned the hard way. When I started mailing my photographs, I put them between two pieces of paper. I was very upset when they came back to me scratched and bent. You can prevent this error by following the directions above. I've found that companies respect your request that material be returned when you send an SASE. Be sure to write your return address on envelopes and packages to ensure their return in case the company has moved or is no longer in business.

Mail Services

You can choose from several options to mail your submissions. For U.S. postal (USPS) mail service types, mailing weights, and rate changes, you can go to the postal web site www.usps.com/consumers/domestic.htm to determine what services are available. Remember to check the Fed-Ex web site for updated services at www.fedex.com and for UPS services at www.ups.com.

<u>U.S. Postal Service (USPS)</u>

1. **First Class** - Regular mail service. This includes postcards, letters, large envelopes, and small packages. Although it is the most expensive way to mail, it generally receives better handling.

2. **Third Class** - Not as expensive as First Class. The delivery takes longer and the handling by the postal service is rougher.

3. **Priority Mail** - Offers one to three day service to most domestic destinations. The envelopes, boxes, labels, and bags are available at no extra charge.

4. **Express Mail** - Offers overnight service to many locations 365 days a year including weekends and holidays at no extra charge. The envelopes, labels, boxes, and bags are available at no extra charge.

5. **Certified Mail** - Provides proof of mailing at the time of mailing and date and time of delivery. The letter or package has to be signed when it reaches its destination.

6. **Registered Mail** - This service is expensive, but it assures careful handling and high security. The item is signed in and out of every post office. Once the package reaches its destination, the receipt is then returned to the sender.

7. **Delivery Confirmation** - Provides date and time of delivery or attempted delivery.

8. **Signature Confirmation** - Provides signature proof of delivery with the date and time of delivery or attempted delivery.

9. **Return Receipt** - Provides proof of delivery. Supplies the recipient's actual delivery address if it is different from what address was used by the sender.

10. **Insured Mail** - Provides coverages against loss or damage for Priority Mail or First Class Mail rates. Items must be insured for more than their value.

11. **Air Mail** - This is very expensive, but delivery could be there the next morning or afternoon, depending upon when the plane leaves for that destination.

12. **International Mail** - You will have to add extra postage depending on the country destination. Ask your local post office. You may have to use a IRC, because U.S. postage would be useless.

<u>Other Mail Services</u>

United Parcel Service (UPS) - This service is somewhat cheaper than First Class regular mail. Any letter you send with the submission, must be placed inside the package. UPS cannot legally deliver First Class mail. The cost depends on the weight of your package and its destination. Services include, next day, second day, third day, and ground (five to ten business days) delivery.

Federal Express (Fed-Ex) - Offers, same day, overnight, or two to three business day delivery. This, too, is an expensive way to mail, yet it is guaranteed to get to its destination within a wide mailing range based on the service you request.

Note: Before you mail your material, be sure to check the greeting card company's submission guidelines for preferred mail service type. Always adhere to the submission guidelines to be on the safe side, even if you have a mail service preference.

-5-

THE PROCESS OF WRITING

Now you can begin the actual writing process. There are three ways to present your verse or passage on a greeting card: 1) a few lines on the outside and a few lines on the inside; 2) one or two lines on the outside and the rest of the verse on the inside; or 3) the whole verse on the inside of the card. If a photograph is on the outside or inside, remember to leave space for the writing (if needed).

Photographs and illustrations should be used to represent the verse. Therefore, you may have to place your verse according to the space available on a photograph. You will also need to be careful that your photograph isn't overbearing or out of proportion for the size of the card.

You should try to place the verse toward the top half of the card because that portion of the card shows when it's in the store rack. Most people will look at a card if it is eye-catching, reading the verse comes after that.

Don't force yourself to write. When the words are ready to be expressed, you'll know because your thoughts will flow easily. There have been times when I had to motivate myself to write by placing myself in an inspiring environment. This will be discussed later.

After you have compiled your work, critique it objectively. Don't be too hard on yourself, yet critique the material honestly. If you feel unsure about what you have done, don't submit it to a greeting card company. It's better to miss a deadline than to submit incomplete or lesser-quality material.

After researching the card market and studying the contents of this book, you can begin your freelance writing. Have all the items you need at hand, then find the right place to write and let it flow.

Getting Prepared

Before you begin writing, I would like to suggest some ways you can spark motivation or inspiration to write.

1. Sit near flowing water or a lake; nature's sounds can create a calming effect.

2. Remain in your home playing your favorite record, compact disc, or cassette.

3. At night, find a place that overlooks the city lights.

4. Sit on green grass in a park or at a college campus.

5. If there is a particular subject you want to write about, put yourself in a similar environment to direct your thoughts.

6. Sit in your favorite chair, close your eyes, and try to imagine a particular event.

7. If you have pictures/photographs depicting a certain situation, examine them while trying to imagine being there.

8. Talk to someone about your particular subject in order to get mentally aroused.

9. There are many other ways to become inspired and motivated. You have to decide what works best for you. Think about it, try it, and let your thoughts occur when they are ready.

Some writers may get a mental block and find it hard to write within any of the above situations or places. If one place or technique doesn't work, try another. You may not have chosen even the right day; therefore, try another day. If you find this to be true, don't force the writing; wait for a better time.

Verses

The following information will help you to better understand and visualize how verses are used for greeting cards.

- Review the verse and passage examples and notice how they would be placed on a card.

- Verse writing can be considered a good opportunity for a writer's self-expression. You can use the opportunity to express a particular thought. The message needs to express a common feeling, because people buy cards to express what they feel or what they want to say to someone. Keep this in mind. If there isn't a meaning in the verse, the card will not sell.

Long verses should have the first few lines on the outside of the card and the rest on the inside. The following two examples would be too long to be placed only on the inside of a card. You should write a note to the publisher, or make a diagram as I have, showing your suggestion about placement of the verse outside and inside the card.

Example 1

Outside
of
Card

> Often I remember
> the times in the past
> of the friends that seemed
> to never last.

Inside
of
Card

> Years had gone by
> before you and I met.
> Although, I admired you,
> my heart wouldn't open up just yet.
>
> I was reluctant to accept
> a friendship that was new.
> But, I could sense
> the sincerity I found in you.
>
> As time allowed the agony
> of my heart to mend,
> I knew that I had found
> in you, a true friend.

Example 2

Outside
of
Card

> To love someone
> is to commit oneself,
> To make sacrifices
> only for that one person
> because no other would be worthy.
>
> To love someone
> is to give of oneself
> in a manner that is special
> that no other will receive.

Inside
of
Card

> To love someone
> is to be yourself,
> To show a side of you
> that no other has ever seen.
>
> To love someone
> is sharing how one feels,
> To try and understand
> how the other feels.
>
> To love someone
> is being unselfish,
> To allow the other
> to grow and love in return.

The following examples are short enough (yet not too long) to be placed inside a card. You may also use these verses as shown per the diagram for use outside and inside the card.

Example 3

Outside
of
Card

> A great distance is between us.
> But, no matter how far,
> my mind often wanders
> with thoughts of you.
> Yes! In my mind, I can see you.
> I even imagine I can touch you.

Inside
of
Card

> I long to hear your voice.
> With every beat of my heart,
> I feel a warm sensation.
> I've put your love within
> a place in my heart
> which belongs to no other.
> My friend, I will love you always.

Example 4

Outside
of
Card

> When I look into your eyes,
>   I feel hypnotized.
> The way you smile at me,
>   it takes my breath away.

Inside
of
Card

> As you gently touch me,
>   my whole world shakes.
> The sound of your voice,
>   takes away my sadness.
> With you, I experience a sensation
>   I've shared with no other.

Another type of verse writing is considered a short verse. This type of verse will always have one or two lines on the outside and on the inside of the card. The outside lines will begin the verse, and the inside lines will complete the verse. When you send short verses to a company, mark them similar to the following four examples.

0) → Outside of Card   **I)** → Inside of Card

Example 5

0) Getting married will be a promising moment...

I)   ... Each moment after that may not be so promising.

Example 6

0) So, you're retiring soon...

I)   ... Now maybe we will get some work out of you.

Example 7

0) I'm sorry to hear you're in the hospital. Don't get used to the food...

I)   ... because when you return, it's back to eating your cooking.

Example 8

0) Let me know if you need anything while you're visiting us...

I)   ... That way, I can give you the list of chores you will need to complete.

Some companies have a preference as to what type of verse they want, and some are open to a variety of ideas from freelance artists. Be sure you know the company's preference.

Passages

Since man has been writing, passages have existed. In early times, passages were usually just a phrase or verse taken from some larger written work, such as a quote from the bible or a philosopher's works.

Passages can be short portions of any written work, from a speech, or a written portion of your own thoughts. Passages are restricted by few rules or limits when used as a short form of free style writing. Often, they may be a few words, lines, or verses, depending on just what it takes to get the point across.

A passage is best kept inside a card. It is used for cards other than the traditional kind. In other words, they are used as inspiring words for nontraditional cards such as best wishes, graduation, promotion, and going away. Look at the next examples.

Example 1

Things are how they are;
but that's not how they must be.
Close your eyes and open your mind;
maybe you will see.

Example 2

Never say a lost cause
is stronger than you.
And don't say you don't care
no matter what they put you through.

Example 3

If step by step is how you take it,
then bit by bit is how you'll make it;
and part by part is how you'll put it together,
if you keep on going through stormy weather.

Example 4

I guess I just wanted to thank you
for all the things you've done for me.
And I'd like to ask if you would help
me the rest of the way through;
and maybe even after that.

Since passages are usually meaningful segments taken from any written work or from your own thoughts, they can and will vary greatly in length and structure. Passages on the average are rather short; it would be unusual to find passages more than twelve lines long. There are few rules to writing passages: they can rhyme, but need not; they can be one line or many; and the subjects are limitless.

Each passage can be used to store portions of personal thoughts and quotes from other works which you have produced. You may also find that writing your own passages for commercial purposes can be very rewarding. Passages can be copyrighted and sold. They are widely used for shirts, mugs, bumper stickers, buttons, and stationery products. Many passages can be used to teach, entertain, warn, or persuade. With passages, you can write as little as you need or to say as much as you want.

-6-

TAX INFORMATION

As a freelance writer, you will be required by law to report all income received. It is up to you to determine whether you are self-employed, a sole proprietor, an independent contractor, or in a partnership. Once you determine your appropriate employment label, it is your responsibility to research what is expected of you by the government in reporting your income and expenses. This Chapter will guide you through the basic law of reporting your income to the state government and the Internal Revenue Service (IRS). You will have to research further for the rest of the information you will need to know to be in full compliance with the law. You can start by going to the Resource Chapter of this book for the contact information.

You need to have an income of a minimum amount each year, in order to file income tax returns. Check yearly with the IRS self-employment tax information to determine what is the minimum amount of income you need to report and the amount of tax you will be required to pay. You may also have to pay self-employment tax, which is separate from federal and state tax.

If you use a portion of your home for personal and business purposes, you may be able to deduct a portion of the expenses on your personal income tax. If you are in a partnership, you would calculate business income and expenses on the partnership state and federal partnership tax forms. Check the IRS web site for more information. The law requires a business to make a profit within a certain period of time before it is considered a business and not a hobby. Save receipts for all your expenses; you will find many items you may be able to deduct on your tax form. The tax forms change yearly. Be sure to check what is allowed to be deducted for a given year. You may find that you can deduct more than what you originally thought.

Don't throw away receipts. Place them somewhere, filed and organized, for easy access at tax time. The more accurate your records are to balance with your receipts, the more valid they will be for tax use. An income and expense sheet or ledger will be of value for tax purposes. You may have to submit a copy with your tax return to the IRS and possibly to the state government.

Tax Laws

After you decide your type of business, tax laws and considerations will apply accordingly. The IRS and the state government have their own tax rules, tax laws, tax forms, and publications. You will need to research both governments for their requirements by visiting the Internet web site (located in the Resource Chapter).

This section will describe the types of businesses recognized by the state and federal government. A few years ago, the state government started requiring businesses to submit a copy of their federal tax returns and supporting business documents with the state tax returns. Pay special attention to the order that the state government wants the documents to be submitted. The state requires some businesses to file a self-employment tax form if they receive income over a certain amount (this will be explained later in more detail).

Make sure you review the IRS and state tax publications and booklets on a yearly basis. Each publication and booklet has a "Changes" or "What's New" section for the current year and the upcoming year. Whether you read any other part of the publications or not, always read the "Changes" or "What's New" section.

The IRS does not require that you have a license or a permit to own a business, but your city, county, or state may decide otherwise. You should contact the local licensing department to determine if you will need a business license and a seller's permit. The city and county are zoned for particular types of businesses. If you plan on selling products (like your own greeting card line), you will most likely need a seller's permit to pay your state sales tax for the products sold. Don't ever assume whether or not you need a license or a seller's permit. Pick up the phone or check on the Internet to save yourself from possible tax fines for not adhering to the business rules. When it comes to running a business, find out exactly what you need to do to be in compliance with the law.

Types of Business

By now, you have probably decided to become a freelance writer, ready to work for a company, or venture on to be self-employed. You may even have decided to go into a partnership with one or two people. What you need to know to be a successful freelance writer or to run a small business will depend on the type of business you pursue. The following descriptions will help you to be better informed about the types of businesses recognized by the government for tax purposes.

Self-Employed - You work for yourself, not considered an employee by someone, and not on an employer's regular payroll. You will be considered self-employed even as a sole proprietor, an independent contractor, or a member of a partnership that operates a business.

Sole Proprietorship - You own an unincorporated business by yourself. You may or may not have a business license. You take the risks of the business. The business has no existence apart from you. You will be able to claim expenses on your personal tax return.

Independent Contractor - This is when you are hired by someone not as an employee, but to be paid by the job or assignment. The person or business that hires you has only the right to control or direct the result of your work, not what will be done, or how it will be done; that is your job.

Partnership - As a member of a partnership, each person contributes money, property, labor, and/or skill, as well as share in the profits and losses. A joint undertaking just to share expenses is not a partnership. You will need to write a partnership agreement to verify and confirm the partnership. Your share of income is part of your personal tax return. The partnership reports the business income and expenses with each partner filing a Schedule K-1 and Schedule SE with their personal income tax for the year. Each partner is responsible for the business profits and losses.

Going into Business

If you decide to design your own greeting cards to sell to businesses, you will be your own boss, make your own designs, no guidelines to adhere to, no editors for rejections, and you have total control of the type of cards to produce. You also need to know that you will be solely responsible for every aspect of the business whether you make a profit or loss. You will be the one responsible for the expectations the government has for self-employed individuals and small businesses.

As the business owner, you need to make some basic business decisions. You need to know:

- the city, county, state, and federal rules and tax laws;
- whether you need a business license, seller's permit, and/or an employer identification number (EIN);
- what marketing strategies to use to sell your products or services;
- what strategic business plan to use;
- the tax forms required by the IRS and the state government;
- the types of business expenses allowed to be deducted;
- how to track business income and expenses; and
- how to track accounts payables and receivables.

When you are ready to learn more about the above information in regards to going into business, go to the IRS Internet web site at www.irs.gov, the small business association website at www.sba.gov or your state's tax web site at www.yahoo.com and type in "individual state tax returns." You will need to locate the link to the state where you are filing your tax return.

Business Start-Up Costs vs. Business Expenses

Business start-up costs are the expenses incurred before you actually go into business. The start-up costs may include, advertisement, searching for an office, conducting surveys in relation to the business, training, purchase of office equipment and supplies, and travel expenses. The start-up costs are considered capital expenses. There may be other start-up costs related to your type of business. The first day you go into business you will be able to recover the start-up costs through amortization. This means you can deduct equal amounts of the cost over a 60-month period or longer. Start-up costs that include certain office furniture, equipment, computers, and buildings cannot be amortized. Those items will be depreciated over a period of time. Get to know the difference between depreciation and amortization. Check the IRS web site for more information.

After you start your business, the expenses are then considered business expenses. You will be able to deduct these expenses for each tax year. Some equipment, computers, and other items that will be in business use more than one year are expenses you will have to depreciate. You will have to deduct a certain amount of the cost over a certain period of time.

You may be able to deduct business-related expenses in regards to business use of your home if you meet the following qualifications as stated by the IRS.

1. The business part of your home is used only for the business.
2. You use the area on a regular basis for business purposes.

And one of the following:

1. Your home office is your principal place of business,
2. It is a place where you meet or conduct business with clients or customers, or
3. You use a separate structure from your home used exclusively for the business.

Remember that you can only deduct the amount of an expense that was actually used for the business. If you use your vehicle for one-half of the business, you can deduct one-half of the expenses for tax purposes. If you use one-third of your home utilities for the business, you can only deduct one-third for tax purposes.

Make it a habit to review all tax publications each year prior to completing the income tax process, so you can stay up-to-date on the laws, requirements, and expectations of the IRS and the state government.

Tax Forms

Along with the personal tax forms you file each year (for the IRS and your state), you may have to file one or more of the following forms as well.

Personal Tax Forms

1099 Misc (Miscellaneous Income) - If you receive royalty payments from a business or work as an independent contractor, you will be mailed this form by the business to add to your personal federal and state income tax forms.

Form 8863 (Education Credits) - If you receive form 1098-T because you are a college student, you may qualify for learning tax credits. Obtain the instructions for Form 8863 to find out if you qualify for this credit.

Self-Employment Tax Forms

The forms described below are to be used if you are self-employed, an independent contractor, or a sole proprietor. You are required by law to pay a self-employment tax if your business income is over a certain amount per year.

Schedule SE (Self-Employment Tax) - You use this form to figure and report your social security and Medicare tax. This form will be submitted to the IRS with your personal income tax forms.

Schedule C (Profit or Loss from Business) - Self-employed individuals will use this form to determine if the business has a profit or a loss.

Partnership Tax Forms

1065 (U.S. Return of Partnership Income) - Partnerships use this form to determine the profits and losses of the business, which will be submitted to the IRS.

"Your state name" Form of Partnership Income - Partnerships use this form to determine the profits and losses of the business and submit it to the State Tax Board.

Schedule K-1 -Partner's Share of Income, Deductions. Credits, etc. - This form will be issued to each partner from the partnership to inform them of their distributive share of the income, profit, and loss of the business. This form is completed for the IRS and the state government.

Schedule SE (Self-Employment Tax) - You use this form to figure and report your social security and Medicare tax. This form will be submitted to the IRS with your personal income tax forms.

The above listed forms are the main forms you will need to prepare your tax returns. There may be more forms for your use, which depends once again on the type of business you have. Always check the IRS and state web sites.

The Watchful Eye of the Government

The government has many rules outlined in a variety of tax publications, as well as on their web site. Every form has instructions either on the form or on a separate form instruction sheet. You can download publications, instructions, and forms from the web site for free. That's one thing the government doesn't charge a tax payer.

It is important that you read all related tax publications before you go into business. You want to make sure that you understand all the rules in relation to your type of business. Contact the IRS or the state government for all unanswered questions or if you are confused about any of the rules, instructions, forms, or publications. If at anytime, you believe a government representative has given you the incorrect information or cannot explain the rules, say "thank you", hang up the phone, and call back later to speak with someone else. I've heard too many times about the government representatives giving out wrong information. Your only other recourse would be to go to a tax specialist and hope he or she knows what the government meant.

Another area of importance is record keeping. The government has rules for why you must keep records, what kinds of records you must keep, how to keep them, and for how long. According to the government, everyone in business must keep records.

Why Keep Records - You need to monitor the business, prepare your financial statements, identify the source of each receipt, keep track of expenses, prepare your tax returns, and as supported documentation for tax returns.

Kinds of Records - You can choose any kind of record keeping system as long as it clearly shows your income and expenses. Your record keeping system should be viewed as the supporting documents in regards to your income and expenses.

How to Keep Records - You need to be able to summarize your business transactions. Journals and ledgers are usually used for this purpose. The record keeping system could include a checkbook, summary of cash receipts, expenses, depreciation, amortization, and/or income and expense sheets.

Time Period Saved for Records - The IRS requires that you keep records for as long as they may be needed (the period of limitation). The period of limitation is the period of time in which you can amend a tax return to claim a refund or a credit. It depends on the incident as to the length of the "period", which could be up to seven years. Check the IRS web site for updated "Period of Limitations." If you have employees, you must keep the records for four years. Keep records for property until you dispose of the property and meet the period of limitations. Records for nontax purposes should be kept longer than what the IRS recommends.

Every year the government performs random audits. As each tax form enters the IRS office, a line-by-line review is performed to determine which ones may be eligible for a more in-depth audit. There is a statute of limitations as to how far back your tax returns can be audited. The state government performs audits as well. In addition, the state government will audit you if the IRS has performed an audit. Just make sure you follow all the rules required by both governments. One way you can stay on top of the rules that change is by reading the front of the publications on a yearly basis in the "What has changed" or "What's New" section. Both the IRS and the state government are reliable in letting you know the changes for the current year.

Contacting the IRS or State Offices

You have several ways to contact the government offices to obtain the publications and forms. It is best to request, order, or obtain the documents toward the end of December because the material is usually in the process of being updated for the tax year. Therefore, you will be mailed the documents toward the end of January or later. That's why it would be much better to download the documents through the Internet, if you have a printer. If you prefer to request forms by e-mail, fax, phone, or pick them up in person, it will still be faster than mailing your requests.

<u>IRS Contact</u>

Internet: Go to the web site 24 hours a day, seven days a week at www.irs.gov. Download or print the documents, forms, and publications.

Phone: Order forms and publications 24 hours a day, seven days a week. Check the web site www.irs.gov for the current phone number.

Mail: You can order forms and publications by mail by using the form toward the back of the 1040 Forms and Instructions booklet.

Fax: Request many of the forms and instructions, 24 hours a day, seven days a week by fax. Check the web site www.irs.gov for the fax number. If you have fax transmission problems, a phone number is also noted on the web site.

Walk-in: Locate your local office in the telephone white pages to pick up forms, instructions, or publications. When the time gets close to tax preparation, you can pick up most of the forms, instructions, and publications located at your local IRS office, post offices, and libraries. You may find some tax forms at grocery stores, copy centers, and office supply stores.

CD-Rom: You can purchase the CD-Rom on the Internet web site at www.irs.gov.

<u>State Contact</u>

Internet: Go to the web site 24 hours a day, seven days a week at the URL address you locate in the front or back of your State Personal Income Tax Booklet. Download, print, or request through e-mail the documents, forms, and publications.

Phone: Locate the phone number in the front or back of your State Personal Income Tax Booklet.

Walk-in: Locate your local office in the telephone white pages to pick up forms, instructions, or publications. When the time gets close to tax preparation, you can pick up most of the forms, instructions, and publications located at your local state office, post offices, and libraries. You may find some tax forms at grocery stores, copy centers, and office supply stores.

Mail: Locate the address in the front or back of your State Personal Income Tax Booklet. Some booklets may have a form in the booklet you can complete and mail in.

Once you receive the forms, publication, and instructions, check to make sure they are for the year you requested. That is why you need to order all documents as early as possible incase you have to reorder them later.

-7-

RESOURCES

Associations and Organizations

In this Chapter, you will find various ways to locate relevant resources for freelance writers. With today's technology, many businesses have web sites. The web sites usually consist of different contact avenues. You may have the option of writing to a physical address, send an e-mail message, or complete a form on the web site and submit it electronically. You can find a majority of the businesses through an Internet search engine, even if they don't have a web site.

NOTE: At the time this book was published, the following businesses, web sites, and general information were current. At any given time a business may close or change information.

Location:
Australian Greeting Card Association
18-20 Queens Avenue
Hawthorn, Vic 3122, Australia

Mail to:
P.O. Box 733
Hawthorn, Vic 3122

Links to professional organizations specifically geared toward freelance writers or other artists - www.freelancewrite.about.com

Gift Packing and Greeting Card Association of Canada
1407 Military Trail
Westhill, Ontario MlC 1A7, Canada

Greeting Card Association of America
1156 15th St., NW #900
Washington, D.C. 20005, USA
www.greetingcard.org

Netherlands Greeting Card Association
Burg. Klinkhamerweg 86a
2761 BJ Zevenhuizen, The Netherlands

The Greeting Card Association
United House, North Rd.
London N7 9DP
www.greetingcardassociations.org.uk

Links to Greeting Card Publishers' Web Sites

www.writerswrite.com/greetingcards/publish.htm

www.freelancewrite.about.com/od/greetingcardpublishers

www.greetingcard.org/gca.html

Links to Freelance Writing Web Sites

Links to online publications that accept submissions from freelance writers:
www.rl44.com

Offers freelance workshops and job opportunities:
www.freelancejobsnews.com

Offers a variety of information for writers:
www.absolutewrite.com/

Online guide to writing of all kinds:
www.writersdigest.com

The business side of writing and making money:
www.writingfordollars.com

Online dictionary, thesaurus, language resources, and more:
www.dictionary.com

References, markets, writers groups, authors, and artists web links:
www.forwriters.com

Resources, workshops, general information, and advice:
www.freelancewrite.about.com

Job opportunities and career resources:
www.freelance-writing.net

Links to greeting card publishers:
www.greetingcard.org/gcassociation_publishers.html

Home business information, advice, and references for starting and managing a home business:
www.powerhomebiz.com

Editorial and freelance services:
www.writecontent.com

Job listings and career resources for writing professionals:
www.writejobs.com

Online community for readers and writers:
www.writergazette.com

Links to books and web sites geared toward writers:
www.writing-world.com

Information about books, publishing, and writing:
www.writerswrite.com

Business of greeting cards and stationery products:
www.greetingsmagazine.com

Publications

Party & Paper Retailer
P.O. Box 128
Sparta, MI 49345
Monthly magazine covering the greeting card gift industry
www.partypaper.com

Poets & Writers Magazine
72 Spring Street
New York, New York 10012
www.pw.org
Bi-monthly magazine specifically for writers of poetry

Reed Business Information
360 Park Avenue South
New York, NY 10010
www.giftsanddec.com
Monthly magazine "Gifts and Decorative Accessories" covering greeting cards, plus more

Writer's Digest
4700 Galbraith Road
Cincinnati, OH 45236
www.writersdigest.com
Monthly magazine for writers

Internet Web Site Self-Employment Information

www.acinet.org/acinet/library.asp?category=2.6

www.artsresourcenetwork.org

www.sbaonline.sba.gov

Search engines** - Type your state name plus individual state tax return.
   Example: California individual state tax return

Use search engines to locate your State's government web site

Internet Web Site Small Business Services

Business office supplies:
www.bizoffice.com

Business information:
www.businessnation.com/smallbiz.html

County business license**
www.(city name)co.business

Federal Express:
www.fedex.com

Own your business:
 preneur.com

Postal Rate Commission:
www.prc.gov

Small Business Association:
www.sba.gov

United Postal Services:
www.ups.com

use the search engine to locate a specific county, city, or state location

Additional Resources

Books for writers:
www.writersdigestbookclub.com

Copyright Office: Library of Congress
                     101 Independence Avenue, SE
                     Washington, D.C. 20559-6000
                     www.copyright.gov

Customs Service Web Site:
www.customs.gov

Internal Revenue Service:
www.irs.gov

International Trademark Association:
www.inta.org

Library of Congress:
www.lcweb.loc.gov

List of greeting card companies with a physical address and a web site if applicable:
www.greetingcard.org

Trademark Search:
www.uspto.gov

-8-

FREELANCE WRITER'S CHECKLIST

This Chapter is to be used as a checklist of things you should review and research in order to be successful as a freelance writer, self-employed, or start a small business. Check which of the following areas you need to research, prepare, or implement, then reread those sections of the book, become proficient in the topic, enhance your strengths, and begin developing your strategies.

Personal Review

Know my strengths and weaknesses and what strategies can be used to compensate for the weaknesses.

Become better organized.

Know what motivates or inspires me to write.

What type of work environment do I need to be productive?

Know how to manage my time.

What type of work schedule do I want and be able to stick to it?

Know how to manage stress.

Know available agency-related resources.

Business Partnership Review

Know what tax forms are required.

Research the definition of a partnership.

Know the pros and cons of a business partnership.

Know the tax laws and legal obligations regarding partnerships.

Research how to write a partnership agreement.

My partner and I need to understand our roles within the partnership and the business.

Business Review

Contact the county or city licensing department to check if I need a business license.

Check with the licensing department regarding the need of a seller's permit.

Do I need a reseller's certificate?

Research the various cards sold in stores; get to know the market.

Decide what style of writing I want to pursue.

Review the copyright law and how to register my material.

Know how to write query letters.

Prepare a model release, if applicable.

Know what copyright form to use and how to complete it.

Know a writer's rights.

Do I need an attorney to review forms and/or contracts?

Research business resources in the community.

Develop a business and marketing plan.

Prepare business card, letterhead, flyers, or brochures.

Decide if I want someone to be a part of my card designs (photographer or illustrator).

Research how to write contracts.

Determine what type of business I want to pursue and research the tax requirements.

Know what mail services are available.

Decide how to arrange and set up the work environment.

If starting a business, know the difference between startup costs and expenses.

Know the difference between depreciation and amortization.

Office Review

Research what type of equipment and supplies will be needed to produce greeting cards.

Decide if I will have a home office or rent office space.

Set up a filing system.

Review and decide what type of computer I need to purchase.

Decide what type of software I need to maintain the business.

Set up a record keeping system.

Develop a ledger for tracking purposes.

Develop an accounts payable and receivable ledger.

Develop a business expense sheet.

Internet Review

Check the Internet writer's guidelines for greeting card companies to request guidelines.

Know how to research the Internet and web sites.

Be familiar with the web sites of interest and those necessary for freelance writers.

Decide whether or not to design and develop a web site.

Know how to use the Internet search engines.

Research business resources on the Internet.

Tax Review

Know what tax forms and publications are needed.

Know the tax laws.

Know how to contact the IRS and the state government for forms, publications, and information.

Know the expectations of the government regarding small businesses and those self-employed.

Know the difference between a hobby and a small business according to the government.

Order tax publications based on my type of business.

Decide if I need a tax preparer.

INDEX

ABOUT THE AUTHOR

Brief Personal History:

- Master of Arts Education (Special Education)

- Educational Therapist for children and adults (private practice office in Sacramento, CA)

  Focus: education, career, and employment guidance and strategies

- Business partner for production of books and music

- Credentialed Special Education Teacher

- Certified Parenting Instructor

- Counsel children, parents, and families (education, parenting, and employment related)

- Family Support Facilitator

Brief Writing History:

- Freelance writing since 1987.

- Five poems published in three anthologies.

- *Freelance Writing for Greeting Card Companies* (the first edition) was written after a two-year study of the greeting card market and was published in 1992. This book is a limited edition and is sold through amazon.com or by the author through B&S Productions located at: P.O. Box 418174, Sacramento, CA 95841.

- *A Woman's Relationship Survival Guide (If He's Worth It)* was written after a three-year study of women throughout the U.S. regarding their relationship issues and was published in 2001. This book sells on the Internet through authorhouse.com, amazon.com, and barnesandnoble.com.

- Other educational, how-to, and self-help books are currently in progress.

Printed in the United States
209741BV00002B/2/A

9 781425 926984